"One believes one is too old to embrace the true spirit of Christmas, and yet it returns with so much power." KAREN BLIXEN

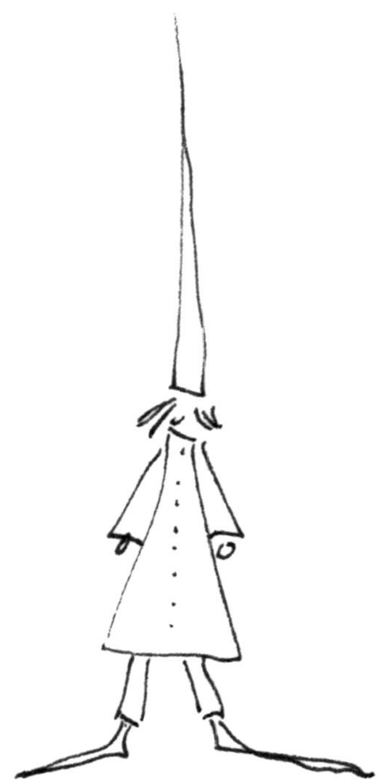

THE CHRISTMAS SEASON

THE CHRISTMAS SEASON

CREATED BY SCANDINAVIAN ARTISTS

Katrine Martensen-Larsen
Photographer Mikkel Adsbøl

ACC ART BOOKS

CONTENTS

PREFACE

Christmas is without a doubt the highlight of the year in Scandinavia. This festive part of the winter season is thoroughly celebrated, gathering friends and family alike on numerous occasions. We are already in a Christmas frame of mind from the first Sunday of Advent, often in late November. Some of us start even earlier, simply because we can't wait. Almost everything symbolises Christmas until it culminates on Christmas Eve (juleaften). This not only applies to us Danes, but certainly also to our Scandinavian neighbours in Sweden and Norway.

CHRISTMAS CHEER

Christmas parties (julefester) are held throughout the month. More often, the ones before the 24th are with friends and colleagues, and those just after - on Christmas and Boxing Day - are typically reserved for the immediate family. During all the Christmas festivities in our respective circles, we bake biscuits, gingerbread houses, Lucia rolls, drink mulled wine and eat nuts, marzipan and mandarins.

On Christmas Eve we unashamedly stuff ourselves! We roast a bird of some sort - whether it be duck, goose or turkey - as well as pork, with gravy, and side dishes of potatoes and red cabbage. Dessert tends to be rice pudding or ris à l'amande, with the added excitement of whoever finds the whole almond receiving this year's almond gift (mandelgave). After dinner, we dance around the Christmas tree and sing Christmas carols. It is only then that we settle down to hand out gifts while dishes of confectionery are passed around. The days that follow traditionally include meals of herring, ham, special sausages, roast pork and jellied meats, washed down with plenty of beer and snaps.

THE DECORATED CHRISTMAS TREE

Some of us go all in with Christmas decorations from the first Sunday of Advent. Others decorate gradually, so that more and more indoor and outdoor decorations sneak in throughout the Christmas period. Lights, stars, wreaths, angels, ribbons, pinecones and flowers, and to top it all, the Christmas tree in all its ornamental glory.

There are as many ways to decorate for Christmas as there are people. Not one way is better than another. It may possibly be said however, that some ways are more tasteful than others. Some go all in to create elaborate nativity landscapes, creating Christmas hearts and making garlands in all colours of the rainbow. Other decorating styles are less over the top and more underplayed. Our book focuses on the latter.

Let it be said right away, you can easily create an elegant decorative home for Christmas without breaking the bank. There is no need to buy expensive ornaments or visit exclusive florists - or even, as some do - hire a professional to create it. Our aim with this book is to show how beautiful it can be, by using pinecones, branches, dried flowers and fewer, but quality, Christmas decorations, in a wonderful mix of old and new, inherited, eclectic, bought and home-made.

A SUSTAINABLE CHRISTMAS

We are well aware that this season especially encourages massive overuse, especially in our part of the world. Thinking sustainably at Christmas is therefore something we are mindful of. We are not advocates of the "buy and throw away principle", whether with Christmas decorations or interior designing.

Bringing Christmas decorations out from storage year after year helps make the holiday season something special. It creates joy for one's self, and certainly also for one's loved ones - especially the little ones. I fondly remember the ornaments my grandmother, grandfather and parents hung on the tree when I was little. I have vivid memories of a small green trumpet and a glass gun filled with pastel coloured sugar pellets. Not to mention my mother hanging socks on my and my little brother's bedroom doors, filled daily with a small gift for each of us, from the 1st to the 24th December.

CHRISTMAS ANECDOTES

A clear recollection is the first Christmas I hosted. My mother lent me her box of Christmas decorations. As I was decorating the tree, I was startled to find that the lametta (ornamental tinsel threads that reflect when the tree is lit) was completely mouldy. Quickly discarded, I then got on with the task of decorating.

My mother arrived that Christmas Eve afternoon and saw our finely decorated tree. It didn't take long before she pointed out that I had forgotten the lametta. I explained that it had become dank, and that I had thrown it away. She promptly burst into tears. What I thought was mould was in fact lead.

You see, the lametta was a treasured possession. It had been passed down to her by her beloved grandmother. Quite simply, it was irreplaceable. Its lead may have appeared slightly dank, but was designed that way so that it could drape heavily and beautifully over the fir tree branches. Alas, this sort of misunderstanding does happen, and it honestly isn't Christmas unless we revisit the episode. I just have to grin and bear it!

THIS BOOK

Within this book, you are invited into twelve homes, belonging to creative Scandinavians. We hope to inspire you, and perhaps even help you evolve some Christmas ideas and techniques of your own. You will see how to make beautiful and imaginative décor by bringing nature into your winter living space, or cutting and pasting using paper, wallpaper and textiles. There will be table settings, gift wrapping, and ornaments. You will see some homes that are considered, and on trend, and examples of some that are quirky, unique and fascinating Christmas havens.

To begin with, you will be provided with a brief introduction to a Scandinavian Christmas. Along the way, I will delve deeper into a variety of Christmas themes. Scandinavia is the geographical area of Northern Europe consisting of Denmark, Norway and Sweden. We share so much - our language and to a great extent also our culture and history. It goes without saying that Danes share a vast majority of Christmas traditions with our Swedish and Norwegian neighbours. There are however small differences. I will naturally be writing primarily from a Danish point of view, but will comment on the differences in Norway and Sweden where relevant.

I have endeavoured to put together a practical and theoretical guide to Christmas, and to create a visually charming work that can be of general inspiration for interior design and styling. At the back of the book, there is a detailed list of the furniture and products seen in the book along the way, and which are available for purchase.

WARMEST THANKS TO

A huge thank you to all of you lovely and creative people, who opened your homes during this holy Christmas season, and shared with us your Christmas traditions as well as recipes for something wonderfully Christmassy which you usually eat or drink during the season. Without you, this book would not have been possible.

Thank you to New Mags who wanted a Christmas book and entrusted me with the task: and to Mikkel, who masters interior and food photography like no-one else I know, jumping wholeheartedly into the concept to spread awareness of our beautiful Scandinavian Christmas to the whole world.

A big thanks also to my sister-in-law, Helene Blanche, for designing such a beautiful print for the book, to Sofia Lynggaard Normann for her illustrative touches, to Sallie Sigsgaard for careful editing, to Becca Shaw Frandsen for great translation work, to Lone Kiær who ran a careful eye over the recipes and to Sophie Klerk for amazing graphic design.

I hope that the contents of the book - text, pictures and illustrations - can inspire you and your family to have beautiful and tasteful celebrations, this year and for many years to come. With heartfelt wishes for a truly Merry Christmas.

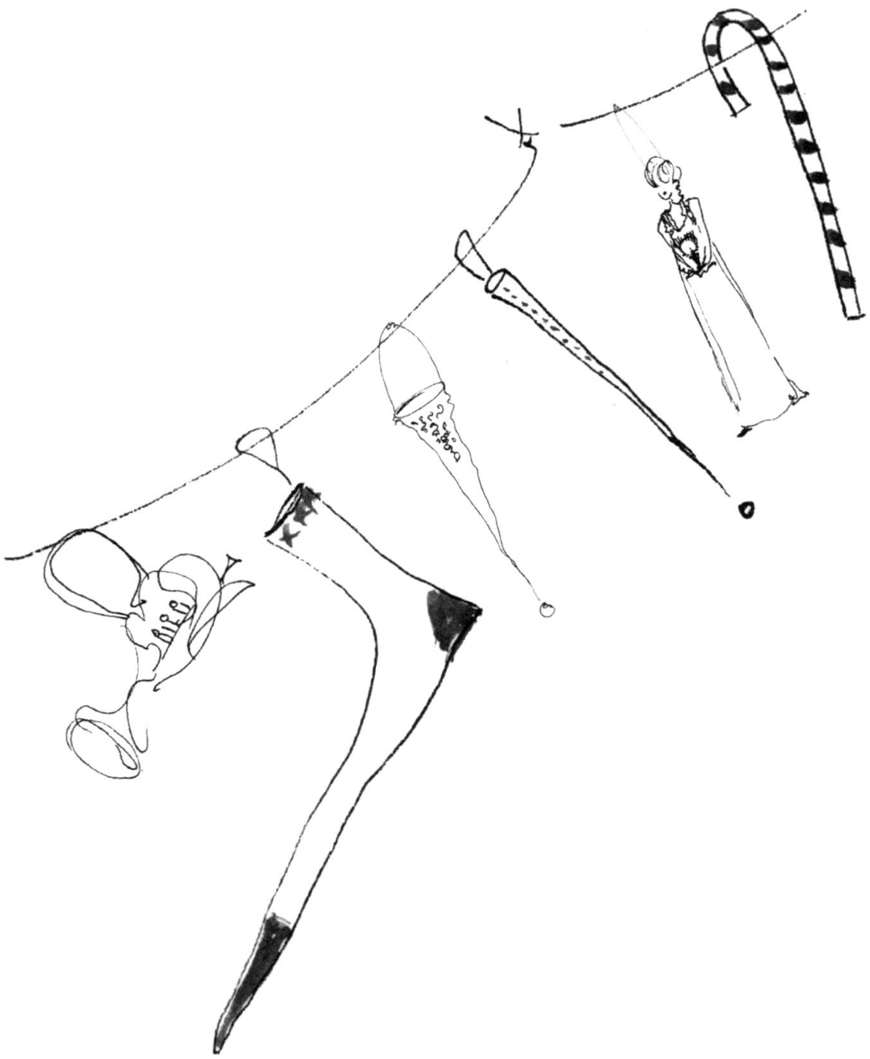

SCANDINAVIAN CHRISTMAS

In the coming pages, and before being welcomed into twelve carefully selected and varied Christmas homes, you can read a little about the background of the Scandinavian Christmas; about our strong Nordic customs - and from where they originate. You will also encounter many of the traditions in more or less newly interpreted forms, throughout the book.

THE FESTIVE SEASON

Originally a pagan word representing feasts, yule or yuletide (jul and juletid) goes back long before the birth of Jesus. It was a festival connected to hunting, and pagan gods. The oldest recorded testimony of Christmas celebrations in the Nordic countries dates back to around 900 AD, when Norway's King Harald Hårfager's son, Haakon the Good, also their first Christian king, proclaimed that Norwegians celebrate jul at the same time as Christians.

MID WINTER FESTIVAL

During the Viking Age, yule celebrations were known as "yule drinking", and were celebrated with ample quantities of food and mead. When Christianity was introduced to the North, the Church permitted this pagan ritual of feasts and drinking to continue, but persuaded Vikings to toast the birth of Jesus instead of Odin and Thor, and to move the Christmas celebration, initially held before mid-winter, to the 25th December.

To follow German and Nordic custom however, the celebrations began the night before, on the eve of the awakening, where together they would wait until midnight, holding a mass to acknowledge the moment of Jesus' birth.

The church clergy strived to abolish the pagan word yule, instead deciding that it was to be called "Christian Mass". They succeeded in England, where the holiday today is called "Christmas". But we Scandinavians kept our "yule" (or rather jul, which is pronounced the same way) with parties, some drinking and plenty of food.

CHRISTMAS TREE DECORATIONS

This first new Christmas Eve tradition initially came from Germany. Germans had already been decorating a fir tree for a century, adding ornaments of paper finery, fruits and candles, and placing a Star of Bethlehem at the top. Since the 1900s, Christmas trees (juletræer) have played a central role adorning almost all Scandinavian living rooms.

The church has also warmly welcomed this tradition with open arms. Since the middle of the last century, juletræer have been brought into churches, and lit during Christmas services. Its symbolism has contributed to many Christmas carols, which are not only sung in church but also in homes throughout Scandinavia, whilst holding hands and dancing around their very own Christmas tree.

WORLDLY INFLUENCE

We picked up the idea of Santa Claus (julemand) and his reindeer from the USA. Christmas cards, roast turkey as part of the Christmas meal, and mistletoe have been adopted from Britain. In about 1930, we started to include the German Advent calendar tradition. Also, in around the 1930s, many people would light a large candle, burning a little each day, to symbolise the lead up to Christmas Eve. It wasn't until 1942 that we produced the actual calendar or date candle that we know today. The Swedes were the first to embrace the tradition of mulled wine and poinsettia plants (julestjerner) - just as they were also the first to celebrate Santa Lucia.

The tradition of visiting Christmas exhibitions and markets dates back to around 1850. By late November, many boutiques would proudly open their decorative and often spectacular displays. It was almost a pilgrimage to visit these exhibits, and children could hardly wait. There would be jubilant throngs of people soaking in the sights and the scent of spruce or roasted almonds, and you could even bump into a real life julemand with his long white beard and clogs.

Nowadays as early as the end of October, Scandinavian interior magazines publish spreads of this year's Advent wreath or articles on Christmassy homes belonging to the rich and famous. Many boutiques, hotels and design houses are revered for their lavish Christmas decoration displays. This year, the internationally renowned Danish porcelain purveyors Royal Copenhagen will be opening its doors for their fifty seventh annual Christmas table exhibition at Amagertorv in Copenhagen. This alone symbolises the start of Christmas for many Danes.

A NORWEGIAN CHRISTMAS

On the lead up to Christmas Eve, Norwegians hang a Christmas star in the window. They bake doughnut cookies (smultringe), ginger biscuits (pepperkaker) and gingerbread houses (pepperkakehuse). Some people drink mulled wine (glögg). The Christmas beer (juleøl) lands in the shops. Many go to family church services on Christmas Eve afternoon. Some visit their loved ones' graves, lighting candles and laying wreaths. In Norway, you also light the Christmas tree after a big Christmas dinner, but not with candles like in Denmark. There is dancing and singing around the tree. Presents are exchanged, and Santa Claus may pay a visit.

The days between Christmas and New Year are known as "romjul" in Norway, originating from an old Norse saying meaning "no need to be holy". Children participate in "julebukke", literally meaning Christmas goats. It stems from an ancient, pagan tradition, where dressed up as elves, they walk from house to house singing Christmas songs and receiving Christmas presents. On the 27th December, Christmas tree parties begin, and julebukke continues taking place until Epiphany or Three Kings Day called "trettenhelga" on the 6th January. Here, the Christmas tree is lit for the last time. Christmas in Norway may be over, but you can still see several Christmas trees standing outdoors until February.

A SWEDISH CHRISTMAS

Sweden also has the ancient festive mid-winter custom where the Christmas goat called "julebuk" is a feature. It is braided with straw to symbolise a new year rich with grain, so people and animals can prosper. On the first Sunday of Advent, many Swedes attend Mass for Christmas prayer with Advent songs (Hosianna). They then light the first of their four Advent candles (adventsstaken) and hang their Advent star (adventsstjärnan) in the window. Some people buy an "adventsgran", which is a small fir tree that can stand on a table. A wreath is made of lingonberries and hung on the front door, and baking is simply a must, especially ginger and saffron bread.

On the 9th December, the Swedes start soaking white fish (ludfisk). It is a traditional dried fish dish, which is soaked in lye and then rinsed. Ludfisk is also eaten in Norway and parts of Finland.

The fabled Saint Lucy's Day of "Santa Lucia" takes place on the 13th December, the Gregorian calendar's longest night of the year. Wearing a headdress wreath of twigs holding four candles in her hair, Lucia leads a procession of other girls wearing long white dresses and carrying lit candles. The beautiful Lucia carol is sung. It represents the comfort of light, and the food and wine are symbolised by trays of coffee, saffron rolls (lussekatter) and gingerbread (pepparkakor). Then from this day, Swedes can start drinking mulled wine (glögg).

Many Swedes attend church on Christmas Eve (julafton) and pay respects at their loved ones' graves by lighting a candle. They manage a hearty Christmas cold buffet lunch and then their Christmas evening dinner.

And so, the Christmas tree is lit, and Santa Claus (jultomten) comes bearing gifts, sometimes even provided with personalised verses to be read out. There is dancing, singing and playing centered around the Christmas tree. The 5th January is called "trettondedagsafton" because it is the thirteenth day after Christmas Eve. This is also called the Holy Three King's Eve. A celebration of when the wise men found the newborn Jesus in Bethlehem and handed him gifts. The 13th January has two names, either the Twentieth Day (tjugondedagen) or Knut's Day (Knutsdag). This is when Christmas decorations are taken down and the trees are removed. There is a song dedicated to this, namely "The Twentieth Knut Day Dances Christmas Away" or "Tjugonda-Knut dansas julen ut".

TWELVE HOMES

The time has come to welcome you to the twelve homes belonging to twelve creative Christmas decorators. The homes, like their owners, are very varied. The common denominator however, is that they have all managed to create a personal and unique Christmas without costing a fortune. They are all artists, or find themselves in a creative universe. They can provide inspiration to create your own beautiful Christmas, and tempt you with some wonderful nibbles or drinks.

TWELVE THEMES

Between each visit, I explore a relevant Christmas theme. You can read more about the origins of our Scandinavian Christmas traditions, such as advent, candles, ornaments, Christmas trees, gifts, Santa Lucia, and not least the great drinking and eating festivities. But let me start by inviting you inside my own Christmas home. This way, you can find out a bit more about me and how I decorate and celebrate Christmas with my loved ones.

MONOCHROME MOODS

KATRINE MARTENSEN-LARSEN

I live in Frederiksberg with my boyfriend Henrik and my two almost grown children, Julie and Jens. Every other weekend, Henrik's two small children, Isak and Selma, also live with us. Our house is one of eight double houses - four on each side of a small road. Designed and constructed in the early 1930s, the houses are functionalist - white, square and practical.

STYLIST, INTERIOR DECORATOR AND AUTHOR

Danish architect Hans Dahlerup Bertelsen designed the eight double houses, with clear references to The Masterhauses in Dessau, Germany. They were amongst the earliest funkis-style buildings in Denmark. Much sought after today, it is said however that when the houses were newly built, with their eggshell yellow facades, red window frames and pale blue eaves and gates, they were simply unsaleable. "No one wants to live in a house like those," they said, which explains why those behind the venture ended up living in half a semi-detached house each. And so, the bricklayer, carpenter and architect lived side by side for many years.

Buying the house in 2016, the renovation task I faced was massive. It was important to me that my boyfriend, who happens to be a craftsman and carpenter, was on board to tackle the challenges ahead. Luckily, he was. After all, the rooms were amazing. There were so many of them, and they were large and regular. The garden is south facing and the property was structurally sound. Other than that, there was little going for it.

The previous family had lived in the house for almost 30 years. They had not adopted the funkis style, choosing to live in an interior with rugs on worn parquet floors, silk curtains and walls painted heavy hues of red and yellow. There were Chinese vases, curved brass handles and ornate radiator covers. In several places, the original beautiful funkis details had been either removed or covered behind recessed ceilings and partitions.

We could certainly see opportunities in this house. After all, there'd be space for everyone and even a nice little garden for our dog. The fact that there was also an underground garage, and a 100 square metre loft extension that could be used as a photo studio and material workshop, was simply the icing on the cake.

The most fundamental change was with the floors. All were removed, and we decided to lay underfloor heating beneath a concrete layer. We thought the concrete would suit this architectural style well, and by laying this subfloor, all possibilities were open in the future. Now that we've moved in, we've grown so fond of the raw expression in the floors, that we probably won't change them.

I was accustomed to living in more classic architecture, but somehow the tighter lines of this house appeal to a more modern and minimalist décor. So, I have slowly evolved from English country style, which was acquired after many years working in London as a marketing manager for Mulberry Company Ltd.

Inspired by the German Bauhaus style in this home - both in terms of furniture and lighting - I try to soften the look with artwork, soft upholstered furniture, soothing bed linen, Moroccan rugs and a touch of vintage. I am the first to admit that there is some style confusion, so prioritise maintaining a soothing colour palette. The same goes for Christmas decorating.

"Before frost sets in, I diligently take cuttings of my hydrangeas, taking them inside to dry. I love floral displays when colours are faded. I also find ivy creepers in my garden, and the long flexible branches of a huge birch tree can be used to make wreaths. It is in nature that I feel most inspired, and often garner my ideas when out on walks with my dog. Flowers and branches can be used in so many decorative ways. Nature is wonderful in the spring when everything is re-born. But something special happens to our surroundings in the fading autumn and withered winter." KATRINE

"During the weeks leading up to Christmas, I begin to gather up long soft, pliable birch branches from the pavements - as many as possible still with their catkins attached. With them I form wreaths, by entwining them around each other, until they have the desired thickness. They must be rustic and simple - not too imposing. I then also cut lengths of ivy and wrap the evergreen plant around the birch branch wreath. Occasionally I also decorate with dried flowers or grasses. I use the same method when decorating the Christmas table, using longer birch and ivy strands. The pretty centrepieces are then used again for New Year's Eve, when I spray them with gold or silver." KATRINE

One could certainly say that my choice of work has a knock-on effect. I am constantly styling and decorating for my clients, and this also goes for our home! So, when Christmas comes along, and our Christmas tree and decorations come inside, compounded by our children's excitable expectations, I find myself in a clash between tradition and modernity. Christmas or not, it must still be beautiful and aesthetic. A career hazard!

It has to be said that I'm not crazy about elves, hearts, glitter, tinsel garlands or bright colours. Santa isn't meant to hang down from our chimney. Wintry landscapes with lakes of mirrors and cotton wool snow on window sills just don't appeal to me. Admittedly when my children were young, they were puzzled, and possibly even a little sad at this, but they have gradually learned to live with their mother's tendency.

When my daughter was seven, she made me a small wooden bird. It was her way of showing me that she realised that if it should ever stand a chance of being displayed, it should be in neutral colours. Even Isak and Selma, with their nonchalant shrugs, show a loving understanding of my design peculiarities. And I am the first to admit how limiting this quirk may seem from the outside. But of course, there must be Christmas - even in my house - and I simply have to prove that tradition and modernity can go hand in hand. And for the record, I simply adore my daughter's bird carving.

Christmas decorations don't have to cost a fortune. For the most part, I use what's in the garden, but I do make a trip to my favorite florist and complement my assortment with that little extra uniqueness. This year however, I did acquire two whole Christmas trees. One is a smaller, pot-grown red spruce from Denmark's forests, which is delivered and then collected again after Christmas so that it can be replanted. I love that idea. The tree now stands, in all its simplicity, in front of our main entrance and welcomes guests.

NORDIC MOODS

dansk
design
HANS DAHLERUP BERTHELSEN

The second tree is a somewhat larger Nordmann spruce, also an evergreen conifer with a broad and cone-shaped form. It stands in the middle of the room, prettily decorated with baubles, birds, stars, paper ornaments and candles - ready for us to dance around it on Christmas Eve. Quite predictably, the Christmas décor has an understated colour palette, so as to blend aesthetically with the rest of the living room.

Unfortunately, the tree is not as sustainable as the red spruce. A Nordmann spruce requires some spraying and fertilizing, to avoid weeds and woodlice. The spraying does play on my conscience. So, in the future we will settle for smaller trees that can be replanted. This is how it should be - even if tradition suggests a Christmas tree must reach as high as the ceiling.

As with many families, ours takes turns hosting Christmas Eve. When it's our turn, I lay the table with my favourite dinnerware and cutlery and wine glasses from Mulberry's Home Collection - given to me by my mother on the morning of my wedding. I used to use the set for everyday life, but some pieces became chipped, and since the set is no longer in production, I now cherish it for special occasions.

"This year, my daughter made this charming Christmas calendar for my boyfriend. In it, were 24 small, edible gifts. He is a massive sweet tooth, so it was an extremely successful present. Placed on a table in our bedroom, it is so decorative, which is also important for the designer in me!" KATRINE

BROWN COOKIES

BRUNKAGER

A generous portion

You will need:

500g salted butter

500g white sugar

250g golden syrup

1kg plain flour

1 tbsp baking powder

250g rough chopped almonds

1tbsp ground cloves

3½tbsp ground cinnamon

Approximately 25g chopped candied citrus zest

Melt the butter, sugar and syrup in a saucepan until you reach boiling point, then remove from the hot-plate and stir in all the spices.

Leave until lukewarm, then mix in the flour and baking powder. Knead thoroughly until smooth, then roll into 4-5 cm thick sausages, then place on baking paper.

Leave the dough to cool (not in the refrigerator) over-night or for about eight hours.

Cut the dough into very thin slices with a sharp knife, or even better using a cutting machine.

When ready to bake, preheat the oven to 160-170 °C, and bake the cookies for 6-7 minutes or until golden brown. Using a spatula, allow the cookies to cool, and when completely cold, place in airtight containers until ready to serve.

ADVENT

This is the period in the church calendar of preparation for Jesus' birth on the 25th December. Advent means Domini, the Lord's Arrival. The church year begins on the first Sunday of Advent - one of the seven dates between the 27th November and the 3rd December.

The year of the Lord begins with a four-week Advent period, where one prepares spiritually to receive the gospel message of the Lord's coming. The four Sundays in the Advent period are denoted the first, second, third and fourth Sundays of Advent respectively.

ADVENT WREATH

A Christmas tradition that came to the Danish town of Haderslev in Southern Jutland from northern Germany around World War I, the Advent wreath or "adventskransen" has a somewhat earlier history. As early as 1900, there were influences from the neighbouring town of Christians- feld, home to the Adventist fraternity. Although known for their Christmas Advent star, they also made Advent wreaths of moss that they hung in their homes.

At about the same time in another town in Denmark called Åbenrå, the wreath became known, but not via Haderslev or Christiansfeld. As the story goes, an elderly townswoman was feeling lonely and distressed whilst her husband was fighting at the Front. Reminiscing about her childhood in Thuringen Germany in the late 1800s, she recalled seeing an Advent wreath with her grandmother.

She visited the gardener in Åbenrå's main street. Not having a clue what an Advent wreath looked like, he then asked an old colleague from Oberschlesia. Luckily he was able to explain. Several Southern Jutland colleagues then adopted this Åbenrå tradition, and by the 1920s, adventskransen became firmly installed as a South Jutland Christmas tradition.

Very soon, the South Jutland adventskrans was to become known throughout Denmark. Florists around the country began creating them in the early 1940s, especially when the celebrity society magazine Billed Bladet did a piece on Queen Alexandrine, who being German, also decorated with an adventskrans.

The candlelit adventskrans was a shining light in a dark winter. In 1946, Christmas postage stamps depicted a spruce wreath with red ribbons and four Advent lights - a true sign that this new Christmas tradition had been introduced as a Danish custom.

ORNAMENTS AND RIBBON

Traditionally, the adventskrans was made by tying spruce onto a straw ring. Nobilis spruce especially was the preferred choice, because of its blue-green hue and durability. Other species such as Norwegian fir, cypresses and cryptomeria pine are also used for adventskranse. Softer branches from witch hazel, willow, euphrases or salix can easily be twisted, then decorated with fresh and or dried flowers, baubles, glitter or anything your imagination allows.

Originally, purple ribbon was used for the adventskrans. It corresponds to the church's Advent colour. Nowadays all matter of colours and ribbons types are used. Or none at all. In the past, they would be hung from the ceiling. Now they can stand on a table and as wreaths. Four candles in a tray is a nice variation on the theme.

The adventskrans has four candles symbolising the four Advent Sundays before Christmas. One of the candles is lit on the first Sunday in Advent. On the second Sunday in Advent, both the first and a new one are lit, and so on. Some are not quite so bound by these traditions, turning on all four lights every Sunday during the lead up to Christmas Eve.

ADVENT STAR

On the 1st December, many people hang a five-pointed paper star in their window, with or without a light in the centre. In Denmark, we call it a poinsettia. It was introduced from Sweden in the 1950s. The Swedes call it the Advent star (adventsstjärnan) or Hernhuter star (Hernhuterstjärnan).

FLOWER POWER

14

LEIF SIGERSEN

An apartment in an old, pale yellow property in the middle of inner Copenhagen, has been Leif Sigersen's wonderful base since 2010. A one room home, just 29 square metres - with a bath, kitchenette, micro dining area, interim workplace, a double bed resting on two palettes, a couple of armchairs, and a wealth of quriosa and treasures - no detail is left to chance.

FLOWER ARTIST, DECORATOR AND STYLIST

Leif's home is living proof that lack of space is of absolutely no hindrance to surrounding oneself with lots of things. From the small tableau creation on a window sill, a charming scene on a shelf or a larger installation mounted on the wall, every single square centimeter is made use of. The contents of this home are a combination of Leif's creations and flea market finds he has fallen for. Flea markets are one of Leif's favourite pursuits, and he frequents them often. Mainly in Denmark and France, but most certainly also when back in the USA. Leif lived in New York for a number of years, once running a high end boutique together with his friend, top model Helena Christensen. Vintage treasures were also amongst the inventory.

Two big busts look out curiously across the street from the window sill. Both are Copenhagen flea market finds, and Leif laughingly calls them Trump and Obama. A giant burnt sulfur matchstick hangs on the wall behind the bed. It had once been a shop installation he designed for Gubi Store. In a corner of the living room stands a majestic swan, which was a supply sale purchase from Royal Copenhagen. To add that Christmassy theatrical touch, it is currently adorned with a gigantic pinecone, and a sparkling star ornament collar. There is no escaping his profession, or artistic talent.

It's not just the fascinating out of the ordinary accessories that are hand picked vintage. All the furnishings in the small apartment are as well. The wall clock for example, used to hang inside an old Swedish watchmaker business. The mid century paintings have been found in various flea markets. Leif created the ceiling lamp, and occasionally replenishes it with new bits. The brown glass droplets were purchased in Paris' Latin quarter. The lounge chairs - also mid century, are Swedish and bought at Helsingborg's antique fair. The 1937 desk chair is originally from a summer house in Tisvildeleje. The workplace shelves were found in a market outside New York, and the 60s tray table is an heirloom. Both hand woven wool rugs date to the 1970s. The brown is Swedish and the one with the yellow figurine once adorned the Danish embassy in Panama.

Small displays of charming vintage Christmas decorations appear everywhere. A pile of colourful antique wooden spinning tops are elegantly arranged on the counter. There are also delightful little cones, created by Leif himself from pages from old adventure books. Leif's handmade Christmas decorations are collector's items for many Danes. In the old days, he sold ornaments such as these from his shop Gaven til Paven (translated meaning The Pope's Present).

There is a funny story behind the name of the boutique. A friend was to visit the Pope in Rome and asked Leif to create a special gift for him. After some enjoyable discussions as to what on earth one could possibly give a Pope, the name for his first boutique was born. This business truly put Leif on the map as a recognized florist.

Leif's love of greenery had been instilled since childhood, and he had dreams of taking over his Godparents' nursery in Dragør. This pleasure was to be short lived however. He found that growing cuttings in a cold greenhouse for months on end was less exciting than he had imagined. Instead, Leif set out to get an apprenticeship with the king in floral artistry - Tage Andersen himself. There was however one small hindrance. Tage Andersen did not take on apprentices.

Leif took all the objections on board, set to work preparing a beautiful application, and arrived on the doorstep of Tage's shop on a Thursday afternoon. The rest is history. His first working day was the following Tuesday, and two years later he was fully trained. A roaring success since, some of the largest international fashion houses, such as Chanel and Isabel Marant are his clients. He is asked to style everything from large private homes to fashion shows and advertising campaigns. It perhaps need not be said that Leif's wonderful table settings have twice been selected to be exhibited at Royal Copenhagen's annual Christmas exhibition.

Space or not, there has to be room for a marzipan pig or two, red bow and all. Leif adores sweet things and explains that he was quite simply put on a fat diet as a child because he was so thin. He was one of those children who could empty an entire Christmas tree for sweets, in one go. His mother only had to look away for a moment - and voila, the tree was looted.

Leif has fond memories of Christmas during his childhood. He grew up in Nørrebro, with his brother and mother. His mother's three older brothers had no children of their own, so Christmases were always with them. This meant that Leif and his brother were well pampered. Not with an abundance of gifts, but with a lot of attention.

Nr. 3

"Limited space does not hinder me from surrounding myself with all the countless significant objects which mean so much to me." LEIF

"This bouquet consists largely of hyacinths, tulips and some spruce. As far as possible, I try to think seasonally, but in this instance I consider tulips and hyacinths to be a Christmas thing. I often feel that an effect is less powerful if you use the same blooms all year round. There is something rather nice about being able to look forward to what the next season has to offer. Where possible, I prefer to create the display directly in the vase, not tied together. In this way there is more freedom and liberal expression. I carefully selected the tulips for their ability to unfurl and reveal their petals. This way, they immediately look like a large open flower in full bloom. To me, a vase is at least as important as the bouquet. A beautiful vase does not require much. A select few blooms, possibly a sculptural branch, can make it look amazing." LEIF

Now, as an adult, Leif takes turns hosting Christmas, with family, partner or friends. Both duck and pork are roasted. But when it comes to dessert, which of course is ris à l'amande, it is not with the traditional cherry sauce. Instead, Leif makes a slightly bitter puree of raspberries with a hint of vanilla, and chooses to boil the rice pudding mix in cream and not in milk. Fret not, you won't be cheated of Leif's own raspberry sauce recipe.

"Even though I love Christmas, I don't always get to decorate my home for the holidays. When you have a knack of decorating for everyone else for months, you have rather had your fill with Christmas when it does finally arrive. But I always try to add some ornaments anyway. In other words, Christmas is an all year round affair for me. I've also made a large portion of ris à l'amande in the middle of summer. I love that dessert." LEIF

RASPBERRY SAUCE WITH VANILLA

Serves 4

You will need:

250g of fresh organic raspberries

2-3tbsp sugar

1 vanilla pod

½dl water

Slice the vanilla pod, scraping out all the seeds.

Place a few whole berries to one side, for decoration. Boil the raspberries in a little water, then add sugar, vanilla seeds and the whole vanilla pod to optimize the flavour.

Simmer for 5-10 minutes and mash the raspberries well. Alternatively use a hand blender.

Serve warm on top of ris à l'amande (cooked with cream, remember), and with a good glass of port.

FLOWERS AND BRANCHES

Floral decorations have always gone hand in hand with festive occasions. Traditionally, living rooms would have been gloriously decked out in luscious green foliage and flowers, to symbolise celebrations, fertility and wealth.

The Scandinavian climate does rather limit the range of natural greenery during wintertime, so we often use branches in our Christmas decorations. In the early 19th century, deciduous branches were left in warm water so as to encourage them to bloom faster. From the late 1800s, improved transport and cultivation methods meant that it was at last possible to buy special Christmas flowers in the shops.

FRESH FLOWERS

Introduced by a French gardener in the 1890s, the first real Christmas flower seems to have been the Begonia. It was about this time that mistletoe made a debut amongst floral decorations in Scandinavia, seemingly adopted from Britain. Nowadays the most typical traditional Christmas flower may be the poinsettia (julestjerne). This is especially true of those with the strong red leaves. They featured on Christmas postage stamps in 1950. In recent times the poinsettia has been cultivated in many other colours.

Displays of hyacinth are also widespread. Many associate its scent with Christmas. Available in many colours, such as dark blue, violet, pink and white, they suit many design palettes. The tulip, another spring flower, has also become a popular Christmas flower, along with the white or burgundy Christmas rose, which by nature blooms in December. The Swedish author Selma Lagerlöf tells a tale of how Christmas Eve turns the forest into a flowering garden to celebrate Jesus' birth. The Alpine violet or cyclamen must also be mentioned - as well as the beautiful high red Amaryllis, which has become extremely popular.

DRIED FLOWERS

Dried flowers and grasses have become a huge hit in recent years. Among my favourites are hydrangeas, which get the most beautiful faded purple and pink colors after just a few weeks indoors. Heartgrass, where the small leaves quiver lightly and charmingly in the light, is a lovely touch.

BRANCHES

Wormwood, cherry, magnolia, fig, larch, holly, coniferous spruce - red, noble, nobilis and sitka, - or pine branches like forest, dune and mountain fir - yes, any branches that have the strength to withhold being arranged in large vases or jars or having baubles, candles and paper ornaments hung from. They can add the Christmas mood long before bringing the Christmas tree indoors, or even be used as an alternative. Softer branches such as silk spruce, eucalyptus, strands of mistletoe and ivy or birch branches are so charming on packages and as wreaths.

WREATHS

The tradition of hanging a Christmas wreath on the door at the start of the Christmas season is indeed a charming one. What a festive way to welcome people and extend the Christmas atmosphere to the outdoors. Many make their own wreaths out of spruce and decorate them with cinnamon sticks, dried oranges, ribbons and glitter. Some choose the simpler look with branches, pinecones and other natural materials.

MISTLETOE

The mistletoe is an evergreen white berry plant, and has over the years been considered to hold mystical and medicinal powers. The white berry is in fact poisonous. Nordic mythology cites that Loki used a mistletoe to persuade Hodes to kill Balder. It was also used to treat epilepsy and to fend off evil spirits and to ward off wildfires. Being a pagan plant, it was banned by the church for a time. Today however, the mistletoe is popular and commonly used as a Christmas decoration.

The use of mistletoe is a common tradition in the United Kingdom and the United States. You see it in many homes for Christmas and Holy Communion, where a sprig of mistletoe is strategically hung high in a doorway or over a seating area. If a girl, young or old (intentionally or accidentally) stands just a moment under the mistletoe, any man, young or old, is allowed to kiss her. Not just on the cheek, but on the mouth. It has also been a sign of friendship in Norse mythology.

Nowadays, mistletoe is an extremely rare plant in Scandinavia, having been slowly eradicated as a weed over the last 100 years. There are now so few wild plants left that they are protected. However, it is found in some private gardens.

SHEAVES

Christmas has been the time for hospitality since the middle ages, and this tendency seems to have grown along with Scandinavia's prosperity. We feel that everyone should enjoy the abundance of Christmas. A visitor to our homes during the Christmas period simply cannot leave again unless they are offered something to eat or drink. Even just a glass of glögg or a couple of vaniljekranse. This also applies to domestic animals, which often received extra feed during this time. There is a Christmas Carol which tells of a dog who gets double as much to eat so that he can tell it's Christmas.

In the countryside, it wasn't only the livestock who benefitted, but wild birds too. After harvest, the last sheaves of wheat were stored, to be hung up on long rods for the wild birds on Christmas Eve. The custom is rooted in the pagan winter solstice festivities, and was a way to show neighbours and passersby that Christmas had arrived at the farm.

By the 1870s, this tradition began to emerge in towns and cities, and is still alive and well today. Not only is it a treat for wildlife during the harsher winter months, but it's very decorative.

COSY COUNTRY

CATHRINE BORGE

We have travelled to Norway to visit artist and boutique owner Cathrine Borge. She lives just a short distance from downtown Oslo, with her English husband Alex and their youngest daughter Lotta. The couple's eldest son, Leon, has moved to Copenhagen, where he is studying furniture design at the Royal Danish Academy of Fine Arts.

ARTIST AND BOUTIQUE OWNER

A warm and smiling Cathrine welcomes us inside their 100 year old dark stained log house - the perfect and archetypal Christmas setting. Initially surrounded by a larger orchard, some land has been sold off, and today it stands near neighbouring houses. We just managed to meet Alex before he left for work, and gather that he is the house's chef, which will soon be evident.

Cathrine, who originally studied Fine Arts in San Francisco, runs Bolina, one of Oslo's most prestigious interior and clothing stores, with her sister, Hanne. The two sisters are the third generation in the Borge family to have the premises, situated at the corner of Stabekks in Oslo. For 40 years, their grandfather and father ran a hardware and pharmacy store in that very spot. Nowadays, it is an exclusive lifestyle boutique for gifts, interior and quoriosa, new and vintage furniture, books, jewellery, shoes and clothing.

The Borge Montgomery family bought the charming wooden house in 2002, and have renovated it extensively over the years. The impressive hallway appears so spacious, with its distinctive white patterned black floor tiles and light delicate matte grey wood panelling. The doors and frames on the other hand, are a crisp high gloss white, to enhance the beautiful carvings and decorations in the woodwork, truly allowing them to shine. A charming little Christmas tree stands in the hallway corner, decorated with baubles and other ornaments.

Another small fir tree stands in a large earthenware pot on the black-painted Chinese dresser. It is completely unadorned, which is also beautiful. A hallway with space for two Christmas trees has an impressive effect. Garlands of fresh spruce are wrapped around the staircase bannisters leading all the way up to the first floor.

It suddenly occurs to me that since we stepped over the threshold, a lovely Christmas mood has overwhelmed me. It's the scent in the house. A delicious blend of cinnamon, eucalyptus and fresh spruce - mixed with notes of citrus and sandalwood from a small scented candle in the living room. The scent is not overpowering by any means - just discreet and evocative. And then there are the comforting sounds from the lit fire in the hearth, providing warmth and adding a cosy ambiance.

In the living room, the distinctive blue / black Italian avant-garde sofa plays confidently up against the two iconic designer lounge chairs of the 50s - both upholstered in leather, one black and the other brown, with their respective wood and steel frames. Cathrine and Alex bought the two distinctive lounge chairs when they first started living together, and they have a genuine touch of patina.

A generous collection of objects, books, candlesticks and vases placed on the coffee table add that pleasant and personal touch. Here too is a charming little box of playing cards - an important ingredient in the Borge family Christmas. Cards are played at any available opportunity during this winter period. Four-man whist seems to be the favourite.

"I may well be completely Norwegian, but many friends would certainly not consider our home archetypal Norwegian. Perhaps it's the colour choice, or the way we display the artwork - for example along the whole stairway." CATHRINE

Sculptures of wood and plaster are placed around the home. They are made by Cathrine herself, from her time at art school in the USA. Cathrine loves to surround herself with art, and the pieces certainly don't have to be her own creations. Although she is a Norwegian, her friends agree that her home is not a typical Norwegian one. Perhaps it's the colours. Or perhaps it's the way she displays her artwork, or even the artwork itself.

The dining room is decorated and the table is set for Christmas dinner. Gift wrapping is taking place in the kitchen, along with decorating the lovely homemade ginger biscuits, with their chalk white icing, pearls and small flowers. They make for super tasty decorations and wonderful host presents during the month of December.

Christmas this year is to be celebrated at home in Oslo, but as Alex is an Englishman with family in Ireland and Scotland, the family often spend the holiday on the other side of the North Sea.

For Alex, on the other hand, baking the traditional English Christmas Cake every year is simply a must. After all, Christmas is not really Christmas without it. Even though we are only in early December, he has been preparing it for weeks, and the cake is still not ready. This personal recipe has been shared with us, but be warned! If you want to enjoy the Christmas cake this year, do start making it well in advance.

THE ALCHEMY OF THINGS
KAREN McCARTNEY

"Norwegians, like the Danes, celebrate Christmas Eve on the 24th December with a big dinner and then we give gifts afterwards. But in England, Scotland and Ireland, we give presents in the morning of Christmas Day on the 25th December. Everyone comes down in their pyjamas- and while we drink morning coffee, presents are quietly unpacked. The children can play with their gifts all day, while we adults leisurely play cards, eat a good lunch, play more cards and then we eat again. It's actually a far better way to do it, much less stressful - at least for families with young children." CATHRINE

"Homemade ginger biscuits, or pepperkaker as we call them, decorated with chalk white icing, cake pearls and small flowers. A perfect host gift during the Christmas season and as Christmas decorations. I bake them every year and enjoy decorating them. I hang the ones I don't give away on fine threads in the kitchen window.

You can easily make the icing yourself but with a pre-purchased one you get that perfect consistency, and that beautiful pearly white colour, which is so important with icing. Bake the cookies at least the day before decorating them, and set aside time for it. If you are busy, the result can be a bit sloppy." CATHRINE

TRADITIONAL CHRISTMAS CAKE

You will need:

250g currants

250g sultanas

300g chopped figs, candied peel, glazed cherries, dates, prunes, apricots (any combination but perhaps not all of them).

150ml whisky

125g soft butter

125g dark muscovado sugar

4 eggs

130g plain flour

½tsp baking powder

½tsp cinnamon

½tsp ginger

¼ - ½tsp nutmeg

¼tsp cloves

50g ground almonds

50g chopped almonds

Zest of a whole lemon

50g chopped crystallized ginger (optional)

Place all the dried fruit into a large mixing bowl, pour over the whisky and stir in the lemon zest. Cover with cling film and leave to soak for three days, stirring daily.

Grease and line a 20 cm diameter round tin with a double layer of greased greaseproof paper. Preheat the oven to 140°C.

Measure the butter, sugar, eggs and almonds into a very large bowl and beat well (preferably with an electric free-standing mixer). Add the flour and ground spice and mix thoroughly until blended. Stir in the soaked fruit. Spoon into the prepared cake tin and level the surface.

Bake in the centre of the preheated oven for about 60-90 minutes, or until the cake feels firm to the touch and is a rich golden brown. Check after 60 minutes, and if the cake is a perfect colour, cover with foil. A skewer inserted into the centre of the cake should come out clean. Leave the cake to cool in the tin.

When cool, pierce the cake at intervals with a fine skewer and feed with a little extra brandy. Wrap the completely cold cake in a double layer of greaseproof paper and again in foil and store in a cool place for up to three months, feeding at intervals with more brandy. Don't remove the lining paper when storing as this helps to keep the cake moist.

TEMPTATIONS

Throughout time, Christmas has been associated with tasty and bountiful food. Initially it was a way to celebrate and give thanks for having plentiful food wares in winter storage, and was distributed to family and guests. In November, animals were slaughtered and preserved (it was in fact formerly known as Slaughter Month). In December, kitchens across Scandinavia would have been a hive of activity (previously known as Bake Month). Also during December, some of the most quality foodwares were saved and stored - both to celebrate jul, but especially to ensure having enough food and sustenance for the cold dark months until spring. It was also a way of symbolising health and prosperity in the new year.

BAKING

Baking bread was the main focus. In the 1600-1700s it was typically round and oval sieve bread (using sifted rye flour). They could be very large indeed (up to 12 kg in weight) and decorated with patterns and figures or even shaped as domestic animals. These loaves were known as Christmas breads and were superior to the everyday coarse bread (baked with unsifted flour). On the larger farms, many hands would be involved in baking produce for winter storage. As thanks for their efforts, the men and women would receive a Christmas sack of baked goods. It was called "julegaver". The priest, the dean, the blacksmith and others from the village also received gifts of bread as a way of a bonus, called "julerente".

In addition to bread, doughnut-like æbleskiver were also made. Since the 1600s, they were often presented during festive occasions all year round, including Christmas. Many today only associate æbleskiver with Christmas, and they are indeed a treat served with mulled wine.

LARD INSTEAD OF BUTTER

Æbleskiver were considered true treats amongst the poorer communities. In many places, men and women were given some to savour at Christmas, and this was considered a great delicacy. Baking æbleskiver was very popular in the past, since the doughnut balls could be made without the use of a stove. They were cooked in saucepans of lard over a fireplace. Before stoves became commonplace in household kitchens, biscuits and sand cakes were largely unheard of. Therefore, the biggest delights of the Christmas season were æbleskiver and a crispy delicacy known as klejner, which are also cooked in lard and do not require a stove.

Butter was a valuable commodity, so fat was often the replacement in most recipes. In Southern Jutland biscuits are still baked using fat. During the roughly 60-year period where it was a part of Germany, preserving the Danish identity was very important. One way to do this was via their food culture, which meant that certain traditions became deep rooted. Gingerbread biscuits were baked using lard instead of butter. There were two varieties, one darker with cocoa and one lighter without. The small ones were served together on a platter.

THE INTRODUCTION OF THE STOVE

The many other types of biscuits we know from the festive season were not really adopted until stoves were introduced into households during the 19th century, and when drinking coffee also became commonplace. In Denmark we bake ginger biscuits (peberkager), vanilla cookies (vaniljekranse), cinnamon biscuits (jødekager) and brown cookies (brunkager).

Norwegians bake doughnuts (smultringe), ginger biscuits (pepperkaker) and gingerbread houses (pepperkakehuse). Both ginger biscuits and gingerbread houses are decorated with snow white icing. The Swedish Lucia rolls, or 'lussekatter' as they are also called, must be baked on the 13th December which is Lucia Day. The rolls are shaped like rounded figures, and are named after Santa Lucia.

NIBBLES AND NUTS

Christmas snacks are first and foremost sweets, chocolates and confectionery, but most certainly also nuts and fruits. The consumption of sweets nowadays is enormous. Not least at Christmas, where the more common sweets are complemented with filled chocolates, nougat, marzipan and other delicacies.

One of the oldest types of Christmas goodies is marzipan, which is a rich mixture of almond and sugar. Originally from Persia, it came to Europe with the Crusaders in around the 12th century. It appeared in Denmark in the 1400s, but it was not until the 16th century, when the first marzipan bakers appeared.

CONFECTIONERY

Marzipan treats are typically small slices of different coloured marzipan layers. Early on, marzipan was also shaped using special wooden cutters. Marzipan pigs were the most popular, and still a well-known Christmas symbol, often used as the almond gift "mandelgave" on Christmas Eve.

Nuts were and still are a common traditional Christmas treat. Hazelnuts and walnuts were harvested, but gradually over time foreign sorts such as brazil nuts and almonds have been introduced. As far as fruits are concerned, we especially see red apples and oranges or mandarins as opulent Christmas fare.

FRUIT PLATTERS

A Medieval legend recounted that apple trees blossomed and bore fruit in wondrous joy of the birth of Jesus Christ. The apple became a symbol of special importance for Christmas. Before the introduction of the Christmas tree to Southern Germany in the 1500-1600s, candle lit apple pyramids were used, and sometimes also more exotic fruits such as oranges and even bananas. They may well be available all year round nowadays, but these fruits still have a special significance in Christmas fruit dishes. The same also applies to dried fruits such as dates, apricots and figs.

SIMPLY SCULPTURAL

CAMILLA ROSÉN

Camilla lives at the top of a beautiful old red brick property, situated in Islands Brygge. It's about 10 minutes walk from Nyhavn, via the newly opened footbridge over Copenhagen Harbour. Here in the charming, almost 90 square metre corner apartment, she and her little dog Bella enjoy a view of the city rooftops.

FURNITURE DESIGNER AND INTERIOR ARCHITECT

One could say that Swedish Camilla Rosén is a bit of a globetrotter. Brought up in Småland in southern Sweden, she trained as a furniture and interior designer at Accademia Italiana in Florence, after which she settled in the Netherlands as Interior designer at the IKEA Concept Centre.

Camilla moved to Denmark in 2008, and started a new job at the Swedish giant. She resigned in 2011, to establish herself as an independent designer. Now at the helm of her own design firm C/RO, based in Nyhavn and founded in 2016, Camilla designs furniture that merges function with sculptural art.

Soaking up so many impressions from home and abroad, Camilla's design signature is a fusion of streamlined elegant lines with generous profiles. Funkis design is a large inspiration, as well as powerful design icons such as Eileen Gray, Coco Chanel, Picasso and Le Corbusier.

The designs are made of glass, stone and recycled steel and are handmade in Sweden. Furniture composed of natural material does not fatigue. It translates just as well outside as indoors. Camilla aims to draw clients closer to nature with sophistication, always applying the underlying motto of quality versus quantity.

Light streams into the corner apartment, on this beautiful December day. We immerse ourselves completely in Camilla's Christmas world and hear of her traditions. A Christmas that can be described in a single word - sustainable.

How exactly is Camilla's Christmas theme sustainable? To start off, Camilla has not spent a fortune at the florist. With the exception of a bouquet of tulips, a few red amaryllis and a single small Christmas rose, the beautifully and elegantly simple indoor decorations are hand-picked from her mother's garden, such as a large fig branch, and bare larch branches with small eye-catching berries.

The large chunky stars are quite simply folded recycled and unpainted paper bags, which Camilla herself has made. Large white Advent stars bid guests welcome at the front door and stand in the large window in the corner room. These are known as Hernhuterstjärnor in Sweden. They were also handmade, using recycled material a few years ago.

Camilla's favourite amongst her Christmas decorations is undoubtedly the seven-armed "Smålandlysestage" that stands on a living room shelf, and was inherited from her grandparents. Her strongest Christmas memories are those spent with her grandmother. They lived on a large farm in Småland, where traditions were kept alive and where Camilla always celebrated Christmas in her childhood.

Everything Camilla's grandmother did was over the top. If it was the table setting it was lavish, if it were meals, they were superfluous and delicate eating experiences, and when decorating for Christmas, it was wildly adventurous. Camilla absolutely loved it. After the death of the grandmother, no-one in the family really kept up these traditions. Her own parents are not quite as preoccupied with Christmas in the same way. Perhaps it will be up to Camilla to take up the mantle.

Ready and waiting and placed on window sills around the apartment, are Christmas presents for Camilla's friends and family members. They are simply and charmingly wrapped in round brown recycled boxes, tied with slim ribbons and with gift cards attached. Beautiful, easy and so decorative. Another circular way to wrap gifts up is to use fabric remnants or pillow cases, and tying the ends with charming bows.

Clearly, you do not need to use wrapping paper. The alternatives are so attractive. After all, it's usually ripped up, discarded and thrown away seconds after the package is opened. Of course, it does rather mean that the presents you give can fit into boxes. Camilla has managed that. Within these parcels are sustainable gifts, such as cinema gift tokens and other experiences, books, and vintage earrings etc.

A delectable platter of Lucia rolls "lussekatter" stands in the kitchen. They are Swedish saffron buns, twirled into S shapes, with the loops wound in at the end. Celebrating Santa Lucia on the13th December with these sweet, soft and golden buns, is simply not one to miss.

"This year's Christmas gifts consist of experiences, books or vintage jewellery. Small things that can be presented in recycled gift boxes." CAMILLA

"I used 11 brown paper bags to make this star. Recycled paper is super. Cover one side of the paper bag with glue, and place a new bag on top of the other. Continue this way until you have enough (7-11). Using a very sharp strong pair of scissors, cut through all the paper bags to make a triangular tip. Pull each side together and you have a star. Fasten the ribbon with a stapler." CAMILLA

"Christmas for me is more about enjoying some relaxing days and pausing from the everyday hustle and bustle. It's about appreciating family time, being around friends, and taking my dog on long leisurely walks." CAMILLA

LUCIA ROLLS

LUSSEKATTER

Makes 25-30 buns

You will need:

50g yeast

175g unsalted butter

Approximately ½g saffron threads

2dl white granulated sugar

5dl milk

½tsp salt

900g all-purpose flour

Egg for the glaze

Raisins as decoration

Crumble the yeast into the mixing bowl. Melt the butter. Using a mortar and pestle, blend the saffron with a little of the sugar, then stir the saffron into the melted butter and add milk. Keep at about 37°C.

Stir the yeast into a little of the lukewarm milk and butter mixture. Add the rest along with sugar and salt. Mix in almost all the flour and knead the dough for about 5 minutes with a blender, or 10 minutes by hand. The dough may well be sticky but be careful not to add more flour, to avoid the buns becoming dry and dull.

Sieve some flour over the dough and allow it to rise under a towel for 30-45 minutes. Knead the rest of the flour into the dough on a table surface which has been sprinkled with flour. Roll into finger-shaped sausages then form into S's. Allow to rise under a towel for 30-45 minutes. Set the oven at 200°C.

Brush with the egg, and decorate with raisins. Bake the Lucia rolls in the lower shelf of the oven for 15-20 minutes. Lay to cool on a cooling tray.

LUCIA

Lucia was a young woman, living in the city of Syracuse in Sicily in 300 AD. Rather than being of the Roman religion, Lucia was a Christian. This was not without its dangers, because the Romans saw Christianity as an enemy of the Roman Empire. Christian inhabitants refused to bring sacrifices to the Emperor, as was the norm at that time.

They were willing to pray for the Emperor and the Roman Empire, but not to worship him as a god. Being Christian was forbidden. You risked being tortured and executed. Therefore, many Christians sought refuge by going into hiding in the catacombs of cities.

LUCIA'S DESTINY

Lucia would sneak out into the night to bring aid and distribute food to the poor. In the dark nights, so as to have her hands free to help, she wore a wreath of candles on her head, to see her way through the streets. When Lucia's mother later miraculously recovered from a mortal illness, Lucia promised to devote her life to Christ and refused to marry the man to whom she was betrothed.

Her discarded suitor took revenge by reporting to the authorities that Lucia was a Christian. She was arrested during Diocletian's persecution of Christians, but each time Lucia was punished for her Christian faith, there seemed to be a divine hand watching over her.

The Emperor banished Lucia to a brothel as punishment, but when being driven away, the oxen would not move. The Emperor then gave orders to burn Lucia at the stake, but the fire would not take. Another legend says that oil would not burn Lucia. This was considered divine intervention.

Eventually, the executioner killed her using his sword. The date of her death was the13th December 304. She was martyred and given sainthood by the Catholic Church. Santa Lucia Day falls on the date she was executed.

SAINT FOR THE BLIND

One legend tells us that to avoid temptation, Lucia ripped her own eyes out. Another says that it was the executioner who stabbed them out. This explains why Lucia is also often seen as a special saviour for the blind or those afflicted with eye diseases. You often see pictures of Saint Lucia holding a small bowl with two eyes lying in it.

LUCIA PARADE

Swedes have celebrated Lucia night (lussenatten) since around the 1600s-1700s. This is especially true in the western part of Sweden, where tradition had it that young girls would wake everyone up at the farms in the pitch-black dark morning, with coffee and specially baked lussekatter, the famed shaped saffron rolls.

The Swedish tradition involving a Lucia procession however is relatively new. It dates back to 1928, when a national newspaper held a Lucia pageant in Stockholm. Now every Swedish city has its own Lucia, who is chosen well in advance of the 13th December. Lucia dresses in a long white robe and wears a spruce coronet wreath on top of her head with lit candles. The procession consists both of girls and boys - wearing long white robes too. The other girls hold a single candle in their hands and the boys (called "stjärngossar") wear a coned shaped top hat and hold a stick with a star at the top in their hands.

Swedes have a wealth of Lucia poems and songs, whereas the Danes only know one, originally about the area of Lucia situated in southern Naples, "Sul mare luccica". The first Lucia parade in Denmark took place at Scala in 1944, which was during the occupation. It has taken off since then, and is regularly part of most Danish schools' Christmas celebrations.

ECLECTIC OPULENCE

HELENE BLANCHE

We visited the home of my sister-in-law Helene Blanche Martensen-Larsen in Hellerup, a suburb north of Copenhagen. She lives here in a white villa from the 1920s with her husband Jannik and the couple's three children, Barbara, Silvia and Johan. They bought the house a couple of years ago, and since then it has received a thorough interior renovation.

WALLPAPER AND TEXTILE DESIGNER

The walls dividing the original dining room and kitchen were torn down, new wide Douglas fir planks were laid, and two new door sections were added at the southern side of the kitchen dining area, to allow for direct access to the garden. The walls are adorned with deep matte colours taken from the entire palette spectrum. Dark petroleum, deep mustard yellow, midnight blue and a delicious putty white.

The colours of the home are a stunning backdrop for the couple's large art collection of unique pieces. Works by artists such as Tal R, Alexander Tovborg, Asger Mortensen, Damien Hirst and Kirstine Roepstorff come to life. In the winter leading up to the holiday season, decorations are made - with the exact same stylish finesse that characterises everything else in the home.

Originally a trained textile designer from Central Saint Martins School of Art in London, Helene met my brother in 2000, just as he had taken over our parents' business in Gentofte. Tapet-Café specializes in wallpapers, curtains and paint. Jannik was in the process of further developing the concept to become the recognized furniture and interior design house it has become today. They now cater for a large prestigious clientele network both at home and abroad.

It is safe to say that Helene and Jannik are the perfect match. It is Helene who successfully designs all of Tapet-Café's own wallpaper and textile collections. Whenever possible, she also fulfills design commissions for other companies.

Jannik and Helene's art composition and colour choices are daring and bold. There is a fusion of Jannik's masculine approach to art and colour choices and Helene's feminine universe of patterns and textiles. The result is a higher entity. It's rare that this can be pulled off so successfully. It requires that the furniture, soft furnishing, lighting and curtains must have the same high finish - and they do.

There is a lot to explore on a single visit, and you can't notice it all. One thing is certain, and that is that the next time you visit, there are new changes to discover. It may be a new artwork, or re-positioned lighting, or the arrival of a new piece of furniture. You will certainly spot new fabrics on pillows or upholstery.

When it comes to decorating the house for the build up to the holidays, it is mostly Helene who gets into gear. Not allowing herself to be governed by tradition, she revels in it. Helene is inspired from year to year, and never fails to surpass herself. She plays with shapes and colours and garners plenty of inspiration from nature. This year for example, she has selected holly and wonderful large branches with charming small red-orange berries. The Danish word for holly is in fact "kristjørn" literally meaning Christ's thorns.

The Christmas table is decorated with glass ornaments and crystals from a family chandelier in need of a renaissance. Separating it into over 50 small parts, she now uses the pieces as decadent and personal decorations, with history attached.

On the other hand, Christmas time for the family is steeped in tradition. First and foremost, all the daily hustle and bustle is reduced to a minimum. The holiday season is for reflection and reconnection. It's time to spend time with the inner circle, those closest to the family. Helene often bakes extra amounts of biscuits, and gives them to neighbours and friends who may not have had the time during their Christmas rush.

For the past few years Helene has immersed herself in painting. She has made large delightful silk cones (kræmmerhuse) which hang on Christmas trees and can be filled with delicious goodies. They are hand painted in ochre yellow and faint olive green hues. They were also exhibited at the Royal Copenhagen's 2018 Christmas Exhibition, when she was one of the designers selected to participate in decorating a Christmas table.

"We do as little as possible. When the winter darkness is upon us, we turn up the cosiness. I spoil the ones I love the most. I also like to go to church on Christmas Eve and we go on wonderful long walks in the woods with our new little dog. As a general rule, we try not to have too many plans during Christmas." HELENE

"It's important to know that these silk cones, or kræmmerhuse as we call them, can be made using all kinds of paper, including old newspapers, glossy paper, even fabric. This is what makes them so unique and personal as ornaments or as gifts. This season, I have used pieces of silk wallpaper that I had left over from decorating our guest room. First, select the size. This cone is made from a piece of paper measuring 23x23 cm. Lay the paper flat and paint your own design of choice. I have painted with ink that I love to work with because of the very intense colour. It also blends easily and you can create the most beautiful effects. When the paper is dry, gently fold it. For glue, I use a strong wood glue. Make sure the paper does not get stains from the glue, so always do a test. For the handle, I used a soft metal thread that is folded in a bow for the hook. Glue the hook to the cone's brim opening." HELENE

Just as with her textile and wallpaper designs, the enchanting kræmmerhuse are magical, and are filled with delicious treats. Helene makes delicious Christmas goodies using her creative magic in the kitchen as well. This year she has baked small Madeleine cakes, adding a bit of sophistication to the recipe with a touch of orange icing and a garnish of finely chopped pistachios. Luckily the recipe has been shared with us.

MADELEINES WITH ORANGE, SAFFRON AND SPARKLING HONEY

Makes 16 large cakes

You will need:

90g butter + 1½tbsp melted butter

2tbsp honey

2 large eggs

75g caster sugar

Seeds scraped from 1 vanilla pod

3tsp of orange zest, finely grated

90g all-purpose flour

1tsp baking powder

Pinch of salt

20g shelled pistachios, finely ground

¼tsp saffron threads

Glaze:

Juice of 1 orange

½cup of honey

Place butter, honey and saffron in a small saucepan over low heat and remove from heat once the butter has melted. Set aside.

Using a mixer, place eggs, sugar, vanilla and orange zest in a medium bowl and beat until all ingredients are combined. Sift flour, salt and baking powder into a bowl and mix into the egg mixture.

Add the butter mixture once it has cooled and mix to combine. Pour the batter into a small bowl or medium jar, cover with plastic wrap and refrigerate for at least one hour.

Preheat the oven to 200°C.

Brush the pan with melted butter and then dust with flour. Ensure that all moulds in the pan are covered, and shake off any excess flour.

Spoon the batter into each mould and bake for approximately 9-10 minutes or until the sides of the madeleines start to brown. If you need to use the mold twice, do make sure that the remaining batter is kept in the refrigerator until ready for use.

Allow to cool for a few minutes and then remove the cakes from the pan. Place on a cooling rack. For the glaze, place honey and the juice of one orange in a small saucepan and warm it up at low heat until it is liquified or very runny.

Brush the glaze over the madeleines shell side up and roll the end of the madeleine along the pistachio pile.

For extra decoration you can add some cake gold dust and mix it with the honey glace. You can also sprinkle it on the top before serving.

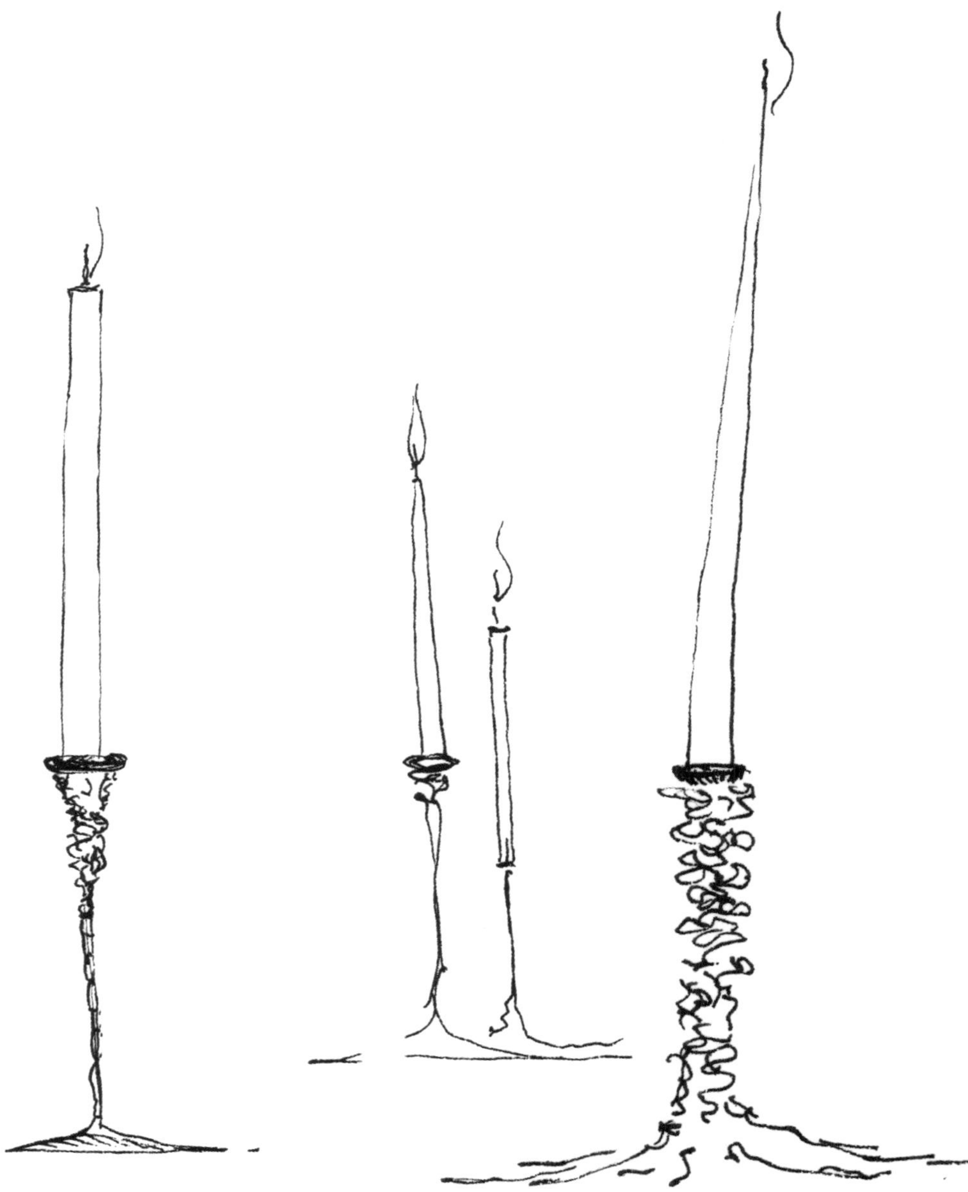

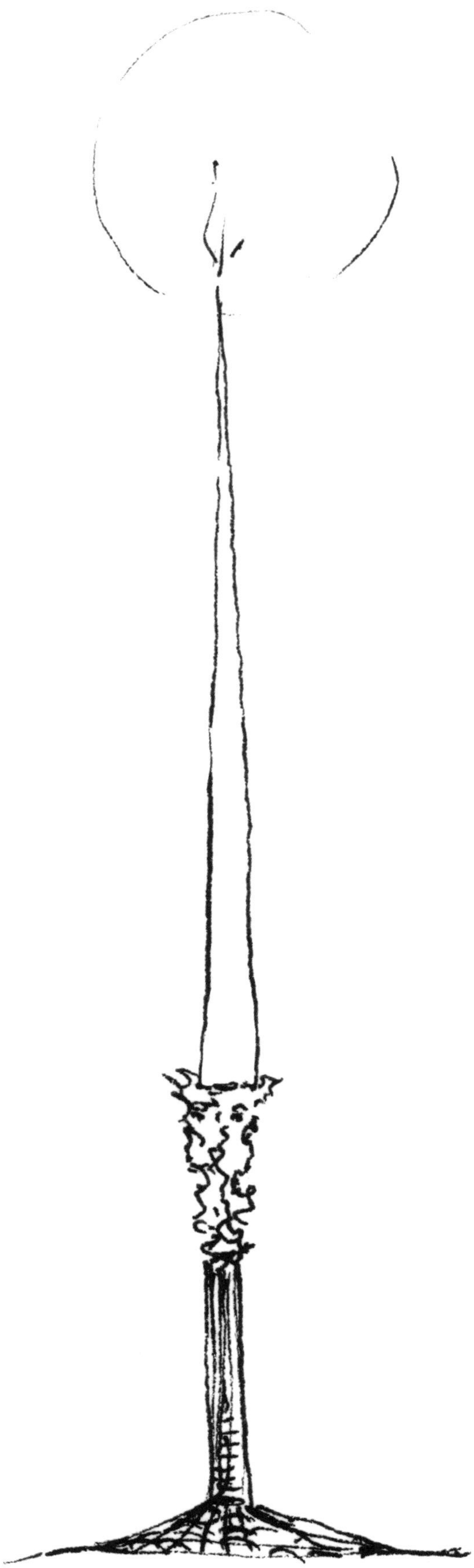

LIGHT

Being the darkest time of the year, Scandinavia's winter months simply cry out for hyggelige get-togethers and candlelight. Wax candles have been a part of Christmas since the introduction of Christianity to Nordic countries. Everyone had at least one candle at Christmas. Candles were cast in moulds, using byproduct from farm animals which had been slaughtered for the onset of winter. In some parts of Scandinavia, they used whale blubber.

Two large Christmas candles stand on the Christmas table during and after dinner and throughout Christmas Eve. Not to be blown out under any circumstances, these were a token homage to Jesus. Often there was a third, larger light placed at a window so that unknown strangers could find shelter in the courtyard.

During Three Kings' Eve and Day, three large candles symbolise each of the kings who came bearing gifts. Occasionally, a special Holy Light candle was made which was one candle with three wicks, so three flames could burn.

SEVEN-ARMED CANDLESTICK

Before Christianity came to Sweden, around the winter solstice, people lit up the cold winter nights with candles. The tradition of lighting mid-winter candles gradually became known as Advent lights. They are alight for the four weeks before Christmas which happens to be at winter solstice and the start of lighter days. Sweden has had their own special tradition when it comes to lights during Advent time and it was not until about 1920 that Swedes started using Advent lights with four candles, to represent each Advent Sunday.

The seven-armed candlestick is a slightly earlier Advent tradition, and is known by Swedes as the Smålands candle - stick (Smålandslysestagen). One can certainly see the connection between this lysestage, and the Menorah from Rome and Judaism. The seven lights symbolise perfection. It was on the seventh day that God completed the creation of heaven and earth. This seven-armed wooden candlestick was "invented" in the late 1800s by a Swedish soldier. Sven August Pohl (1859 - 1934) carved one for his manor house Fällan in the parish of Dannäs in Småland. The family used it for Christmas, and upon seeing it displayed in Jönköping in 1900, the local county museum purchased it for 25 kroner. The money was probably much needed, as Pohl had been disabled that same year in a blasting accident which had robbed him of his sight and damaged both his hands and lungs. Pohl's candlestick has since been copied and developed in many different varieties and is now popular worldwide.

ADVENT CANDLES

As elaborated earlier in another chapter, the Advent wreath tradition of four candles came to Denmark from Germany in the 1940s. Its four candles symbolise the four

Advent Sundays before Christmas. One of the candles is lit on the first Sunday in Advent. On the second Sunday in Advent, both the first and a new one are lit, and so on. Some are not quite so bound by these traditions, lighting all four candles every Sunday during the lead up to Christmas Eve.

CALENDAR CANDLE

Calendar candles are one of the newer Christmas traditions that have become widespread since World War II. However, there is much evidence that different, more "popular" types of homemade calendar candles existed before then. You could very easily draw stripes on a normal candle, after all. In the 1930s, many people bought a large candle, and decorated it as a calendar candle. The first factory-made calendar candles could already be purchased during occupation, when the candle maker Asp & Holmblad began to make calendar candles also known as date candles.

FAIRY LIGHTS

Nowadays almost all homes have outdoor light decorations, and strings of light shine in the night sky from the end of November and often until January. Fairy lights are wrapped around windows and front doors, balconies, porches, and even chimneys. Indoors, they adorn bannisters and eaves. Some choose lights of all colours of the rainbow, but I feel the most beautiful type are the yellow fairy lights. I usually decorate some larger trees or bushes in the garden and pot plants on the balcony.

Many also use the thin light strands with LED lights indoor, to avoid live candlelight and the potential dangers of them. It is convenient for a number of reasons, not least reducing fire risk. The LED chains are wrapped around the Christmas tree or around various Christmas decorations, and in window frames or door frames. Your imagination is your only limit.

TREE LIGHTS

In Denmark, it has been a tradition to have live candles on the Christmas tree. After Christmas dinner on juleaften, the tree's candles are lit behind doors, then the doors would open to reveal the glowing lights of the juletræ, to delight both children and adults alike. Many have a bucket of water standing in the living room corner just in case.

Swedes and Norwegians rarely use candlelight in their trees, considering the fire danger to be too great, especially as many of the houses are built of wood. Instead, the tree has been lit by electric, or more recently LED fairy lights.

SUSTAINABLE PLAYFULNESS

SHANE BROX

Much of Shane's working life has been devoted to projects for children and adults alike to be inspired to tap into their imaginations. Born in Canada, hence the English-sounding first name, Shane moved to Tromsø in northern Norway when he was three. Here in a valley surrounded by snow-capped mountains, elves and the magical Northern Lights, he lived with his Norwegian mother, Danish father and two younger brothers. Shane now lives in the heart of Copenhagen, overlooking the stunning King's Garden.

CHILDREN'S AUTHOR, DESIGNER AND STORYTELLER

Shane has been obsessed with building, drawing and designing houses, since he was very young. Sometimes they were enormous, on several floors, and full of rooms, including plenty of secret ones. Outwardly, everything seemed idyllic, but dramatic happenings unfolded within these houses - and in Shane's imagination. In fact, Shane was so fascinated by secret hidey holes that he even had one. As a twelve-year-old, he quite simply sawed a hole in his bedroom wall. His unsuspecting parents only discovered this several years later, when they were remodelling the family home!

He developed a fascination for the fall of dynasties, crumbling ruling houses of yesteryear, and beauty losing its luster and disappearing into oblivion. Other children played with Lego. Shane built with homemade wooden blocks, dolls and bits and pieces. He still does.

A highlight of the year in Shane's childhood was Christmas time. At home they would bake, prepare, preserve, store and organise. It would begin in late November, with a huge house clean from top to bottom, including the rehanging of curtains. Then gradually during December, they would then cut and glue and create decorations, until this Norwegian home was beautifully and lovingly decorated throughout.

Every 23rd December, the grown-ups decorated the large Christmas tree, and on the morning of the 24th, the three brothers would each wake up to a red Christmas stocking with a gift inside. This very same stocking hangs from his bedroom door in his home. In the afternoon, the family would pay a visit to the snow-white cemetery, where they would light candles by their loved ones' graves. A custom from their time in Canada, they ate roast turkey for Christmas Eve dinner, and dessert was ris à l'amande, seeing as Shane's father was Danish. Later in the evening, they would dance around the festive Christmas tree and exchange gifts.

Shane left Tromsø at the age of 18 to commence his artisan and design education at The Design School in Kolding, Denmark. It wasn't just houses, palaces, fairy tales and mysteries that fascinated Shane. He was captivated by tales of ancient Hollywood, and its glamour, extravagance and decadence. Upon graduation, Shane landed his dream job as global trend spotter for Levi's, and investigated subcultures in places such as New York and Tokyo. It would appear that Shane had found his niche in this trendy underground environment. Beneath the surface however, he felt as though there was something lacking. He seemed to be more and more drawn to nurturing parts of his inner child. Shane needed to explore this strange fantasy universe in his mind, and find ways to express it through art, writing and creativity.

The new millennium had barely rung in when Shane started to write children's books. This led merely a few years later to a television programme for Denmark's Radio. The Shane's World series inspired children to use their imaginations and make fun bits and pieces out of recycled items that would otherwise be discarded. He gave children the ability to see new opportunities and breathe new life into seemingly worthless things. This programme was Shane's breakthrough.

Shane has created and designed varied assignments over the years. For example, he designed a children's porcelain dinner set for Royal Copenhagen in a revival of all their classic porcelain figurines. As previously mentioned, the world-renowned Danish porcelain house Royal Copenhagen, has a wonderful annual tradition of inviting famous artists to decorate Christmas tables. Shane has had the honour of being invited twice, each time creating imaginative and lavish arrangements. He was commissioned to create a ballet for the Royal Theatre, writing and designing the fantasy ballet Fabelmageren (The Fable Maker) for the children's troup. For two years, he was trusted with special access behind palace doors, and was able to discover what four generations of the Danish royal family had stored in their attics. Then in collaboration with the Queen's art historian, Shane selected the most interesting and spooky things out of their dusty hiding spaces, and designed a 700 square metre exhibition at Amalienborg, pertinently entitled 'From the Royal Attic'.

Shane feels that children must be motivated to set their imaginations free, be true to themselves, be curious, and to take a stand for the world around them. Recently, he conceptually developed and designed the large exhibition "Our World" at the Natural History Museum in Aarhus. Here, he interpreted the UN's 17 World Goals, to make it easier for children to understand and perceive the bleak environmental and climate challenges facing the world today. His exhibition managed to convey the seriousness of the situation, in a quirky, fun and informative way.

Currently working on an exhibition in the ruins under Christiansborg Castle, dating back to Copenhagen in its infancy in the 1100s, Shane is constructing great monsters, silly monsters, angry monsters and troubled monsters, based on children's emotions and medieval aesthetics.

Shane's life mantra revolves around reusing what we have in new and creative ways. His interior design style also involves this principle of giving old pieces a renaissance. Most pieces can become fantastic with a creative makeover. Everything in the charming old apartment is either inherited, cloned or a second hand find. The sofa is the one exception. Made especially for him more than twenty years ago, it is in fact due for a creative transformation. Shane would like to spruce up the sofa cover with a patchwork of saved fabric swatches in grey muted tones, artfully sewn together with bright yellow thread.

There are bits and pieces waiting patiently to be given a new life. Like the wry smiling elves, some bedraggled dolls, or a primitive vintage homemade toy warship from the 1950s. In fact, it was from precisely these three items that Shane created this year's Christmas tableau, "Make love not war".

A soothing backdrop is required to envelope items of such a variety of colours, shapes and sizes. Shane painted the apartment in three ultra-matte shades of grey. From dark, darker and the darkest of all, the further into the home you come. The walls, the frames, panels and doors are all painted in the same tone, to create tranquility. It is extremely atmospheric and demonstrates the control that Shane has mastered, namely being creative both in the children's world, but in the adult world as well.

NORDISK
VÄRLDS
ATLAS

Greta Thunberg

"I love brown recycled cardboard. I build everything out of it - large exhibitions, toys and this year even Christmas decorations. I make big stars for hanging in windows, on doors and as table place cards. I also make large Christmas figures. Everything from angels, to Christmas kings and snow queens. It's such fun to see some of the original cardboard print, as it tells a story. And I always add a bit of sparkle, so it isn't too boring. I'm crazy about glitter, and until I find a good sustainable version, I'll use what I have in stock." SHANE

"I have grown up with the Christmas tree as a pivotal part of our Christmas. Now however, I have chosen to say goodbye to this tradition. It's hard to reconcile the fact that a tree has to die just because it has to stand in my living room for a few days, then be thrown away. And with regards to presents, I wrap them in brown paper or newspaper, and then decorate them playfully and beautifully with things like recycled silk ribbons, old Christmas ornaments, toys, and pickings from the forest. I don't use tape. Everything is put together with a glue gun." SHANE

"My Christmas table this year includes a naughty group of red wine elves. They are made out of used corks, which probably explains why they are such troublemakers and all over the place when skiing. They drink too much, play too much music, throw up and roll around in the snow!" SHANE

GINGER BISCUITS

PEBERKAGER

Medium sized portion

You will need:

625g plain flour

200g dark brown soft sugar

200g salted butter

125g golden syrup

1¼dl cream

1tsp bicarbonate of soda

½tsp ground pepper

½tsp ginger

½tsp ground cloves

½tsp allspice

Pour the butter, sugar, syrup and cream into a thick-bottomed saucepan and cook for a minute. Stir well, then allow to cool.

Mix the flour, spices and bicarbonate of soda together, and pour in the mixture. Knead the dough, divide into smaller portions and allow it to rest overnight in the refrigerator before rolling it out.

The next day, pre-heat the oven to 200°C. With a little dough at a time, roll it out as millimetre thinly as possible on baking paper. Stand in front of an open window so the dough stays as cold as possible while working with it.

Cut out the dough into shapes using cookie cutters. Bake for 6-8 minutes at 200°C.

Garrish with sliced and halved almonds, fixing them with a little egg white. Bake until golden brown, a little depends on the thickness of the cakes.

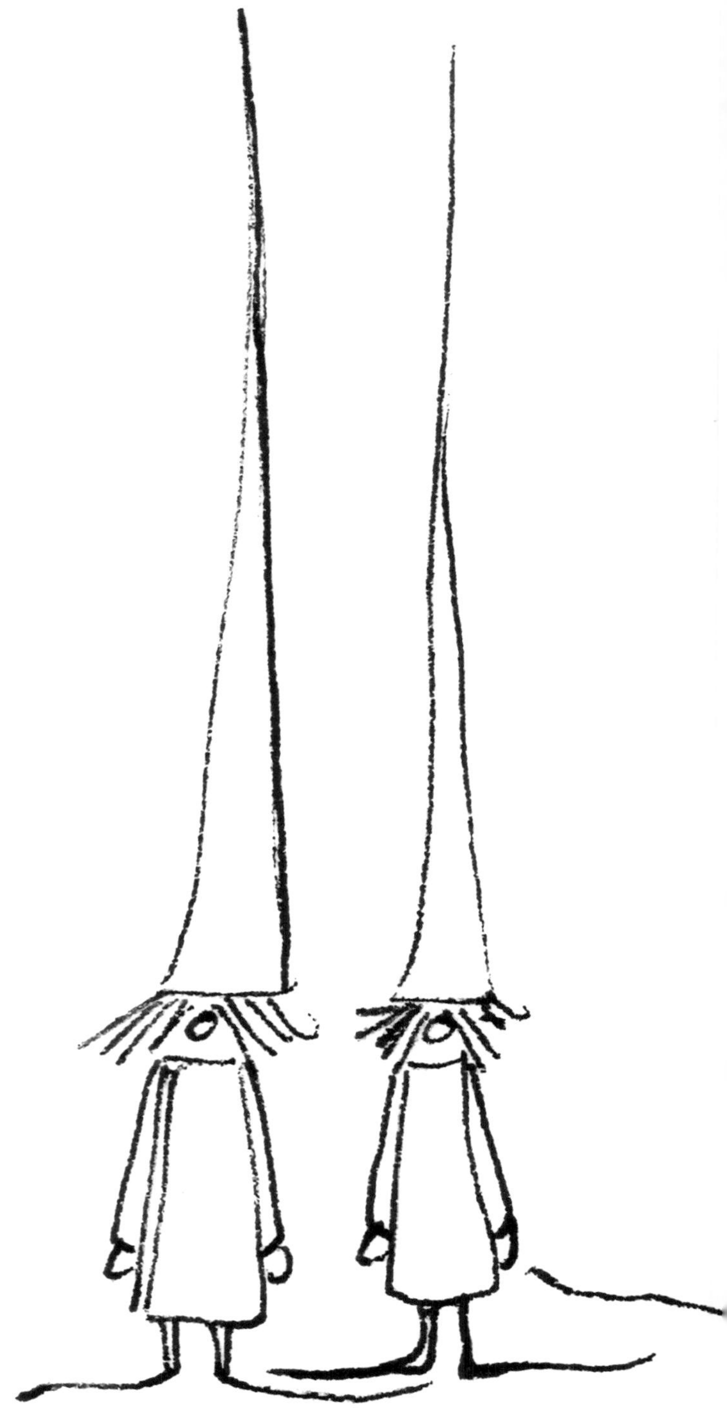

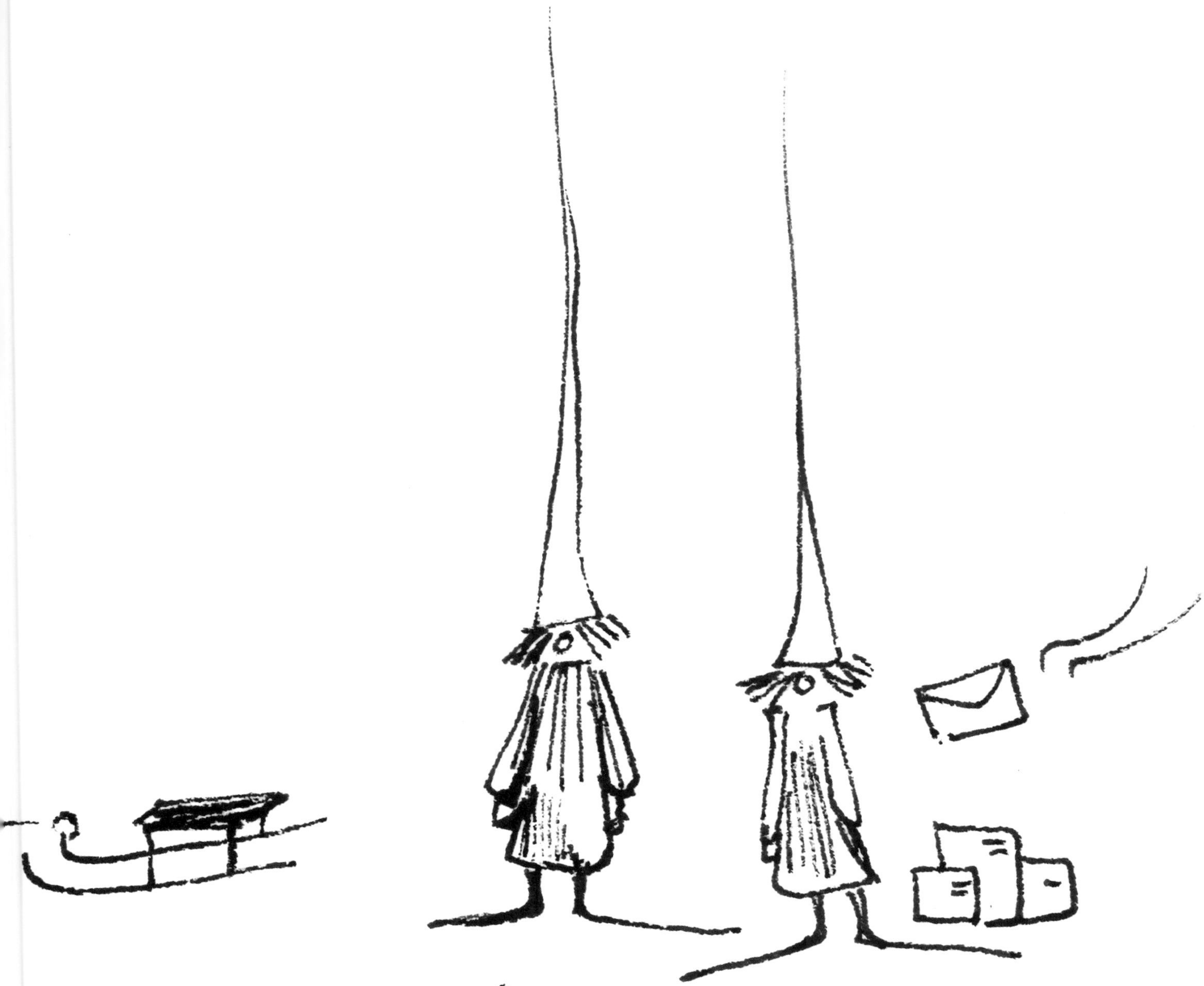

FIGURES

Nowadays, elves and Santa Claus are possibly Scandinavia's most popular Christmas symbols, but we most certainly also come across a number of religious figures during this time. The main ones are taken from Christmas nativity and biblical tales of Jesus' birth. The three Wise Men and the Star of Bethlehem originate from the Gospel according to Matthew, while shepherds and angels are from the Gospel according to Luke. The bull and the donkey that lie beside Jesus are probably derived from the 600-year-old scripture Pseudo-Matthew Infancy of Jesus Gospel.

There is evidence that the nativity has been a part of the Christmas celebration since the 800s, but it is more than likely that this tradition emerged around the 600s. Nativity plays were made popular by Francis of Assisi, who in 1223 created a Christmas manger in a cave dwelling in the Italian city of Greccio. The story of Francis of Assisi's nativity scene gained popularity and became a custom throughout Europe. The tradition disappeared in the countries which experienced the 16th century Reformation, and this included Denmark, Norway and Sweden. It was not until the early 1900s that nativity returned and is now firmly established as a regular custom.

ANGELS

According to the Old Testament, angels are God's servants, acting partly as messengers, partly as pious protectors, and occasionally to convey punishments from God. Evidence from writings in the early Old Testament suggest that angelic powers evolved so the supreme ones ranked as archangels, cherubs and seraphim. Some were even given names.

Needless to say, angel imagery is a widespread church art form. They can be categorised as seraphim, cherubim, thrones, dominions, virtues, powers, principalities, archangels and guardian angels. Each group forms an angelic choir. Both majestic seraphim and cherubim have several pairs of wings, often studded with eyes. Winged angel heads on chairs are cherubims. Sometimes they are seen as being four headed. They can wear blue and white fairy shirts, headbands, and robes. Their hands are raised, sometimes with flaming swords.

The third ranking thrones are seen either as fire charioteers or as people with their hands in prayer, with headbands and eyed wings. Dominions, virtues and powers are white robed, with green shawls and cassocks. They have sceptres, golden girdles, and can bear crowns, and powerful rods. Principalities wear similar robes, but have footwear. They are more gladiator-like. Their left hand rests on their chest, and they bear a lily in their right. Archangels and angels are white clothed and winged. There are seven archangels; the most frequently mentioned being Gabriel, Michael and Raphael.

Angels are often depicted as trumpeters to symbolise their role as God's messengers. Other imagery includes wreaths (victory of Christianity); lilies (innocence); musical instruments (heavenly music); palms (victory); passion; swords (guardians of justice and good) and walking sticks (messengers). Angels should be youthful and genderless. Church imagery however does not always meet these criteria.

THE HOLY THREE KINGS

Traditionally, three wise men were referred to as kings as they came bearing valuable gifts. According to a medieval legend, the three kings were named as Kasper, Melchior and Balthazar, and journeyed from afar from each corner of the globe, signifying Jesus' birth was for all.

Unlike the popular Scandinavian Christmas song: "Now it's Christmas Again", Christmas does not last until Easter according to church teachings. However, it is still very much celebrated until the Epiphany or Three Kings' Day.

If you wish to heed this custom, decorating for Christmas can only take place immediately before Christmas Eve, and then it is all taken down for Three Kings' Day. On the 5th January in the evening, it's time to eat the last of the Christmas goodies, and light the three-armed Holy Trinity candle.

ELVES

The Christmas elf (julenissen) is a supernatural being, dating back to Viking times. A little old bearded man, who dresses in grey knitwear and trousers, wears a red hat and socks and black clogs. He has a penchant for his yearly Christmas pudding, and brings presents for the children on Christmas Eve.

Every farm had an elf, and he was to be respected. If you weren't kind, he would tease you. You made sure to remember to leave rice pudding out for him, or you wouldn't get any Christmas presents. There are several kinds: forest elves, dunes elves (slightly larger than the forest ones), garden elves, farm elves, wall elves (mainly resident in old historical houses), and lastly Siberian gnomes (resembling trolls, and larger than European gnomes).

DANGLING ELVES

In 1947, the Danish cartoonist Frederik Bramming invented the dangling elf. Drawn on sheets of cardboard, they were designed to be cut out and used as Christmas decorations. The sheets were produced at an art publishing house and were a great success. You can still buy them today. They are called Brammingnisser, and can be found as puzzles, Christmas socks, napkins and various Christmas ornaments.

SANTA CLAUS

The myth of Santa Claus is based in part on Saint Nicholas, the bishop of Myrra in Lycia in Asia Minor (Turkey) back in the 300s. Saint Nicholas had wealthy parents, but was known for distributing help to the needy. Legend has it that the bishop's neighbour, struck down by one terrible accident after another, saw no other way out, but to sell his three daughters as slaves. He went to the bishop for advice, who suggested he pray night and day. Three times, large bags of gold coins fell down from the attic. The poor neighbour could now keep his dearly beloved daughters. Nicholas became known as the children's protector until the 18th century, when he was sainted.

Julemanden is a mythical character, who hands out gifts to well behaved children on Christmas Eve. He has many names: Santa Claus (USA), Father Christmas (England), Jultomten (Sweden), Julenissen (Norway), Babbo Natale (Italy) and Weihnachtsmann (Germany). The Santa Claus myth is especially popular in the USA and Germany (from where the legend started).

Santa Claus is a large, rotund man, with a long white beard and a resounding, hearty laugh - Ho Ho Ho. On Christmas Eve he sets off on his reindeer driven sleigh with Rudolf in the lead, and hands out gifts to children of all ages. He manages to enter the homes by landing on roofs and crawling down through the chimneys, and places the gifts under the tree or in Christmas stockings.

If there is a treat set out for him, he eats some of it. Since he drops in to all children around the world, that's a lot of food. No wonder he's a little round. For the rest of the year he resides in his workshop with his busy elves (and Mrs. Claus), preparing and making the gifts. There is some discussion as to where Santa Claus actually lives. Places such as Greenland, the North Pole, Turkey, Finland and Russia have been mentioned as possibilities.

SEASIDE PEACE

CHARLOTTE LYNGGAARD

Backed on to the shelter of the forest and elevated above the sea, it's hard to picture a house situated more sublimely. We are visiting jewellery designer Charlotte Lynggaard, who with her husband Michel, and the couple's youngest son Julius, lives a little north of Copenhagen. The couple's two oldest daughters Sofia and Laura moved away from home recently, but fortunately still often come and stay for weekends.

JEWELLER AND CREATIVE DIRECTOR

Charlotte and Michel have painstakingly transformed a small former summer cottage over a number of years, in a true labour of love. A feat of good luck and perseverance meant that they managed to get their hands on the property as newlyweds, gradually changing it into a wonderful New Hampshire style villa. Magnificent views of Øresund (the Sound between Sweden and Denmark) are all encompassing, with its several balconies, covered porch, multi-level terracing, split level interior plan, and bay windows.

Trained as a goldsmith at Ole Lynggaard Copenhagen as a young woman, Charlotte has been an integral part of the family business ever since. For a number of years, she was even the outward face, modelling for several of the company's image campaigns. Today, she and her father are responsible for all the collections as well as the company's visual identity. There is no doubt that Charlotte has been a decisive factor in the company's great success. However, she is quick to add that she certainly cannot take all the credit.

Both her husband, brother and sister-in-law are intricately engaged in the business, and the parents still play a very important and visible role. The company has flagship stores in Copenhagen, Stockholm, Paris, Sydney and Singapore, in addition to selling wholesale to dealers around the world. The Lynggaards have chosen to keep control of the company and are involved in all processes - from design, material procurement, production, sales and marketing.

Charlotte and Michel's home is luxurious, yet utterly unpretentious. Here, we see a fusion of carefully selected quality building materials with good decorative classic design choices. An example of the successful mix of new and old is in the living room. Here, a new, bright and sleekly designed Italian sofa is softened by two padded armchairs, one solid block colour, the other with a larger blue pattern. They are both heirlooms from Michel's grandmother, and reupholstered by Charlotte.

A lovely mixture of oil paintings, watercolours, drawings by renowned artists as well as Charlotte's own collages adorn the walls. Several small plaster figurine sculptures of women in graceful positions are placed around the living space. Michel is beginning to explore his artistic avenues, and long may he continue, because they are charming.

The exterior of the house is clad with cedarwood, and the roofs are a dark matte tile. The elegant doors and windows, with their ultra-narrow rafters, are painted in an appealing faded green, blending beautifully with the ivy climbing randomly over the facade. The flooring indoors has natural tiling from the Swedish island of Øland, and Douglas fir planks in the study and large open kitchen. These are merely two examples of the delightful materials used. As testimony to the age of the house, and its humble beginnings as a summer cottage, one can see that the original rooms still have the narrower floorboards. Preserving the home's history is a charming detail.

"December is arguably the busiest month of our year, but we take time out of our schedules to appreciate the wonderful Christmas month, and I make an effort to decorate the house and create a cosy home. It's important to enjoy a quiet moment of contemplation for myself on the porch, cup of tea in hand, to soak up the meditative and wonderful view of the Sound. It's good for the soul." CHARLOTTE

The house has certainly undergone transformation and grown in size over the years. But rather than choosing to initiate a massive encompassing building project, Charlotte and Michel have taken a different and more organic approach, and extended the home gradually in stages, in line with the family's needs over the years.

As we enter the courtyard, three tall fir trees stand proud, like brave guardsmen, welcoming us to Christmas. If you have plenty of space in front of your house, it is a super idea to get your Christmas tree (or rather in this case Christmas trees) a good while before Christmas. They can be enjoyed for a lot longer, and be brought indoors a few days before the 24th December. Stepping inside, one can see other examples of nature in the decor.

It is abundantly clear that it is not only when designing jewellery that Charlotte taps into her creative side. This is clear during Christmas time too. She combines her innate stylish aptitude and deep understanding of material compositions and colour. Rust red and vintage pink witn touches of green/blue petroleum hues, and selected cuttings from charming old paper bags, silks and velvet ribbons, characterise this home's Merry Christmas.

Charlotte's large dining table stands in the middle of the equally-oversized kitchen and is sumptuously decked out for Christmas. It is covered in vintage coral cloth, and every surface is decorated with elves, red apples, tureens, jugs, tealights in coloured glass holders, pinecones and the Holy Three Kings. They are all sitting amongst the entwined and elongated strands of ivy draped down the middle of the table.

The place settings are family pieces, adding authenticity and tradition. These include a porcelain set with delicate floral designs, crystal stemmed glasses, coloured water tumblers, and cutlery with bamboo handles matching perfectly with the pale wood chairs and table. Each place has a pale coral napkin, tied together with homemade ribbons, and decorated with individually cut figures. A spice cake is placed on the table (a recipe from her grandmother). Looking almost as tempting, are two pies, pear and apple respectively. Overlooking the scene, and ensuring peace and harmony, are white angels and paper cones, hanging from invisible threads.

The planned opulence of Charlotte's Christmas table has clear references to Sweden's much-loved Carl Larsson. There is a decided contrasting calm in the living rooms. Of course, there are still Christmas decorations, but in a very discreet way. Most notable is the extremely large Advent wreath hanging above the coffee table in the middle of the living room. It is a wrought iron creation, embellished with dried branches and simple white lights. The wreath was made by a blacksmith several years ago and can be decorated a little differently from Christmas to Christmas.

Two tempting glasses of hot white glögg, figs, chocolates and a platter of large homemade vaniljekranse are on the coffee table.

A vase of evergreen rhododendron branches stands on a console in a corner of the living room. Next to it are three glass baubles, purchased from one of Charlotte's favourite boutiques, Stockholm's Svenskt Tenn. The workbench between the living room and kitchen is a creative hub, almost a paper workshop. It is here where throughout the month of December, paper cuttings and decorations are made, and presents are wrapped. Charlotte stores gifts in baskets or in a charming large coarse linen sack that hangs on the kitchen bannisters.

"My napkin rings are cut by hand, but you can choose to make a template first to make sure that the length is long enough to fit around the napkins. Draw the ends the way you'd like them. You can sketch leaves, runes, flowers, spirals - anything your imagination comes up with. Cut out the template and pencil it faintly onto the paper of your choice. Then cut it out and lastly make a small slot which holds the ring in place around the napkin." CHARLOTTE

"I simply can't bring myself to throw pretty paper bags and boxes away. Instead I save them and use them in all sorts of ways. I cut out gift cards, ornate shapes for the table settings, and make napkin rings to go with the coral hued napkins I embroidered." CHARLOTTE

SPICE CAKE

KRYDDERKAGE

You will need:

125g butter (room temperature)

2 eggs

200g brown sugar

2tsp cinnamon

1tsp ground cloves

1tsp baking soda

Zest of a whole lemon

100g raisins

50g chopped candied peel

1¼dl semi-skimmed milk

250g white flour

Stir the butter and brown sugar well together. Beat in the eggs one at a time. Mix together flour, cinnamon, ground cloves, baking soda and the grated lemon zest. Add in the milk gradually, whilst stirring. Then finally add the raisins and candied peel, until it all becomes a dough.

Bake the cake for approximately 45-55 minutes in a greased cake tin at 170°C. Insert a fork in the centre to test if it's ready. It should come out clean.

FEAST

It is believed that the first Christmas feasts during the Viking era served pork. During the slaughter month in late November, fatted healthy pigs were driven home from their rich forest habitats, so that the meat could be cured and stored. As previously mentioned, some of the best quality pork was set aside for Christmas.

PIGS AND POULTRY

Before roasted ham or pork was served on Christmas Eve, a festive platter of a well garnished pig's head was brought in ceremoniously. One would also feast on medister and blood sausage, and all sorts of ways to serve a newly slaughtered pig.

In the 1800s, around the same time that gifts, Santa Claus and the Christmas tree were introduced, there was competition as to which meal was served. Townsfolk started eating goose instead. In the countryside however, pork or the occasional slaughtered duck was the most usual dish. It was in the late 1800s however, that roast turkey made an entrance. Nowadays, the classic Danish dinner menu consists of roast duck, turkey or pork, with caramelized browned potatoes, red cabbage, waldorf salad, red currant jelly and gravy.

In Sweden on the 24th, a sumptuous cold Christmas lunch of herring, salted meats, sausages, pork and Christmas ham is served. That very evening, the Christmas dinner consists of ham, ludfisk and rice pudding with almonds. Norwegians also eat rice pudding and almonds, but start with pork or sheep spare ribs. and goose, turkey, or meat roast, boiled cod or halibut.

PORRIDGE

Porridge has been a fixed tradition for every family's menu since they started celebrating Christmas at home. Everyday porridge was made with water, using barley or rye, but during the Christmas season it was cooked with milk. It was not until the late 1800s that Christmas pudding was made using short rice cooked with milk. It was around then that rice started being imported. Everyone could buy it at the grocery shop, although it was still considered a luxury in the countryside.

ALMOND RICE PUDDING (RIS À L'AMANDE)

Once the availability of rice was widespread in around 1900, a new and more exclusive variant emerged. Rice pudding started being mixed with chopped almonds, whipped cream and vanilla. This resulted in ris à l'amande, from the French "riz à l'amande" meaning rice with almond. Despite its fine French sounding name, it is an entirely Danish invention. Ris à l'amande retained its exclusive status until just after World War II. Nowadays it's more popular than rice pudding.

ALMOND GIFT

Eating porridge for Christmas is a tradition that goes back hundreds of years. The custom of putting a surprise whole almond in one serving, with a prize to the person who finds it in their helping, comes from 16th century France. Here it originates from the celebration of the Three Kings, where the "Prayer King" was the one who found a prayer, coin or a small figurine in their so-called "King cake". The Prayer King was given the privilege of determining the day's festivities.

In Denmark, the almond and almond gift dates back to the 1600s, but the custom really only became widespread during the 1800s. Initially, the prize for finding the almond was that something special was granted - ie. a privilege just like the French Prayer King. It could even be the first to marry (unless the almond was bitter), being allowed to kiss that special someone on the mouth, or having a wish fulfilled.

Since the late 1800s it has become more common having an actual gift as a prize. In the past, the almond gift (mandelgaven) was likely to be a sweet treat, such as the beloved marzipan pig. It was also popular to give various humorous cartoon booklets. Today however, all kinds of mandelgaver are given. For some strange reason, it's very often children who find an almond in their portion.

LAVISH VIBES

Madam Tofte's Gaard
Anno 1755

CAMILLA AND SOPHUS GETHER

We are visiting Camilla and Sophus Gether inside a historic timber framed townhouse, at the back of Madam Toftes courtyard in Nyhavn, old Copenhagen. Here, high in the eaves, in a spacious 160 square metre penthouse apartment with a balcony and roof terrace, they live with their little son Vincent. Camilla got her hands on this amazing loft space a few years before she met Sophus, and together they have lovingly renovated it.

ART DEALERS AND COLLECTORS

The family have now lived in Nyhavn for eight years, and although they are well aware that it's just a matter of time before they will need more space, it is difficult for them to imagine a better home. The apartment is not only ideal, but it's situated perfectly. Quite simply, they don't have a bedroom for Vincent, who is currently living in what used to be his parents' dressing room. And while it's super cozy, it's just a matter of time. And oh dear, when that time comes!

The first thing you notice when you step straight into the apartment from the elevator, is the open flow of handsome and wide Douglas fir planks, the many crooked lines, sloping angles and exposed beams. Then the art catches you off guard. During this festive time of year however, it must make way and allow decorations and the Christmas tree to steal the limelight.

The couple's personal art collection stems from artists represented by their gallery, and their countless professional travels to art trade shows around the world. Camilla and Sophus select pieces as often together as they do separately, and wherever they happen to encounter artwork they fall for. They do not always have to agree, but certainly respect each other's choices and opinions.

Sophus' first visit to an art exhibition was at just three weeks old. It is not completely off base to say that he was raised in the art world. His father is director of the Arken Museum of Modern Art just south of Copenhagen, and his mother was a senior curator at the National Gallery of Denmark (SMK). It is safe to say that art was a hot topic in Sophus' childhood home.

Art has also been a large influence in Camilla's upbringing. Both her parents have been avid art collectors throughout their lives, always having a deep and passionate interest in art and culture as a whole. As a family, they have paid numerous visits to museums, galleries, art fairs and theatres around the world.

After working at London's White Cube and Haunch of Venison galleries, then later at Galleri Susanne Ottesen back in Copenhagen, Sophus set up his own gallery Gether Contemporary in 2014. Situated in Copenhagen's hip meatpacking district, it is dedicated to new and international contemporary works that pushes the borders of how one perceives art. Relatively quickly, Gether Contemporary has become one of the most important Nordic galleries to showcase new young talents on the art scene.

Camilla has helped behind the scenes, and been a sparring partner since the gallery's inception. She took it a step further in 2018 when she left her previous career to take a job as Fair Manager for Copenhagen's new annual International Enter Art Fair, which takes place at the end of August.

Camilla had already started to decorate their home in late November. She visited her parents' home in the north of Copenhagen, and brought back three long cherry tree branches. On the 1st December, she brings out her Christmas ornament boxes from storage. Every single charming piece is neatly wrapped and packed away. This is the time of year when they can come alive.

The branches are carefully decorated, but many of the ornaments and all the candle holders are reserved for the Christmas tree. Some of the oldest pieces date back to her great-grandmother, who came from Christiansfeld in Southern Jutland. The adorable little winged windmill crafted in Dresdner cardboard is but one example. Treasured ornaments that have been passed down to the fourth generation always bring joy, a smile on the lips and wonderful memories.

"Christmas is a special time of the year in our family, because we get the chance to slow down the hectic pace a bit, and spend time immersing ourselves in each other. Our Christmas is not standardised. We truly value the unique Christmas ornaments in that they are personal and tell a story about us, our journey, and our history as a family." CAMILLA

Camilla also selects new ornaments every year, from Christmas markets abroad, or boutiques in Copenhagen, gradually widening her collection. There is a special place in her heart for antique birds. Once the branches are decorated with baubles, stars, pinecones, birds and cut out figures, they are neatly hung in the window sills.

As December progresses, the Christmas tree takes up residence in its usual place in the bay window, which is wallpapered with a familiar little pattern "polka squares" a playful interpretation of the classic polka dot. The tree is charmingly decorated and here, in a little hiding place, sits an elf "nisse" - knitted many years ago by Camilla's grandmother. She also made the nisse family, nonchalantly occupying the Børge Mogensen Spanish Chair.

"Every year, on the last weekend of November, I visit my parents and forage in their garden. To be more specific, I tend to aim for their large cherry tree. I cut three branches of about two metres in length - preferably some with many small shoots. Back at the apartment, I find all my Christmas decorations, attach thin red silk thread at the end of each branch and add the birds, before I hang the branches in the window sills. We have two in the living room and one in the kitchen. Once the branches are up, I decorate them a bit more with selected ornaments." CAMILLA

Camilla hasn't just adopted the family Christmas decorations from her mother. She and Sophus also now have the tradition of hosting Christmas for parents, siblings and children. The family attends a Christmas Eve service at Garrison Church in the afternoon of the 24th December. Afterwards, they return to the apartment where they fuss over the cooking together, and diligently discuss which wines to drink. The family always cooks together, but one thing is certain - it is always Sophus' mother who makes the traditional ris à l'amande.

RICE PUDDING AND ALMOND RICE PUDDING

RISENGRØD AND RIS À L'AMANDE

The Gether family has a tradition of eating rice pudding on the 23rd December, what we Danes call little Christmas evening (Lillejuleaften). They eat it with butter and cinnamon sugar.

Serves 4-6

For rice pudding you will need:

180g short grain rice

1l full cream milk

3dl water

1 quality vanilla pod

75g castor sugar

A pinch of salt

Rinse the rice well and bring the water and rice to a boil in a thick-bottomed pan. Cook the rice under even heat, stirring for about 2 minutes. Add the milk and bring to a boil on a high heat, stirring constantly.

Split the vanilla pod and scrape out the grains. Add it all into the rice, with sugar and salt. Simmer on a low heat for about 4 minutes. Stir regularly. Remove the vanilla pod.

Put a lid on the pudding you are saving for your ris à l'amande, and place it in the refrigerator until it is cold. Preferably overnight.

For ris à l'amande you will also need:

100g blanched almonds

4dl whipping cream

Amarena cherries

Cook, peel and roughly chop the almonds. Whip the cream until it forms soft peaks. Gently fold the chopped almonds and whipped cream into the rice pudding.

Refrigerate for another three hours. For those who have the almond gift tradition, push one whole almond into the pudding. It should be well hidden.

Serve with warm and cold Amarena cherry sauce, and a generous glass of port.

DECORATIONS

As we all know, Christmas is not just about Christmas Eve and Christmas Day. The period leading up to the holiday season is a special time of preparation, expectation, socialising and having fun. This is why our homes are decorated throughout the Christmas season. But that moment the Christmas tree is brought indoors and is tastefully decorated, is a special moment indeed.

CANDLE HOLDERS

The oldest Christmas decoration is the candle. Last century, animal fat lights or wax candles were used, and were attached to branches with needles inserted through them. In around 1870, one began to experiment with clamped candle holders. German manufacturers would attach small reliefs of baubles, birds or angels in varying colours. Other clamps were wrapped in gauze and swivel ball bearings. Later on, the weighted rod candle holder was used.

EDIBLE CHRISTMAS DECORATIONS

Other early ways to decorate included gingerbread men, pastries, and chocolate figures. Marzipan shapes came a little later. These were all edible treats that could be nibbled after dancing around the Christmas tree. As it says in the song, "High from the Tree's Green Top"; first display them, then eat them!

CARD AND GLASS DECORATIONS

During the 19th century, Christmas ornaments from Germany, Bohemia and the Czech Republic caught on. First arrivals were the most beautiful figures, crafted in great detail from Dresden cardboard and later on in glass. These included baubles, bells, Christmas angels and countless other figures. They were made by skilled glass craftsmen using artisanal traditions in Bohemia and southern Germany. The hand-blown glass forms had thin layers of silver added inside. Only then would the outer shell of the figures be hand decorated with colour and glitter. Nowadays, cardboard and glass ornaments of that era are expensive collectibles.

PAPERCUTTING

Towards the middle of the last century, paper decorations became a part of the Christmas theme. In homes across Scandinavia, ornaments of all shapes and sizes were cut and pasted in glossy, patterned and tissue paper, sometimes with more enthusiasm than talent. Various designs were made, the most usual being cones, and small baskets. They would have been decorated in festive colours and patterns. Both were ideal to put goodies inside. Woven paper Christmas hearts also appeared, along with paper chains and garlands. Flags and drums were first introduced towards the late 1800s.

FLAGS

In Denmark, and after the The First Schleswig War of 1848-50, the flag became quite a bourgeoisie symbol, and the flag of the people. That tradition is still very much alive today. This is why Dannebrog is so widely flown in gardens and allotments across the land, for birthdays, celebrations, anniversaries - which surprises our foreign guests.

When Southern Jutland voted to re-affiliate in 1920, a national revival spread throughout the country, and it became fashionable to adorn trees with numerous flags. The occupation of 1940-45 certainly didn't hinder this tradition. Nowadays however, this tradition has a strong divided opinion. Either a tree simply must have flag garlands, or it's absolutely not the thing to do at all.

TREE TOP

Most Danish Christmas trees today have a star on top. After all, the Star of Bethlehem guided the three wise men to baby Jesus, so there is certainly strong Christian symbolism.

However other figures such as Christmas angels or Santas cut out with a front and back, so they're easy to slip on, have also been used in the past. Storks were also popular to celebrate Jesus' birth.

One can still occasionally find icicles, made of coloured or silvery glass. These seemed to have been popular for Christmas trees in circles where the star's Christian affiliation was not deemed appropriate. Special metal tree top decorations similar to the popular chiming angel ornaments can also be used. These are metal ornaments with a number of candles, which when lit, would create heat to turn the mobile, sometimes causing a chime.

NATIVITY SCENE

Certainly, one of the most traditional Christmas decorations is the nativity scene of the old church, with baby Jesus in a manger, the Virgin Mary, Joseph, shepherds, animals, angels, three wise men, and the Star of Bethlehem. By the 1600s, this practice had spread to most Catholic churches, and from the 18th century onwards, people started to include nativity scenes in their homes.

ELVES

Elf landscapes of all types, in different activities, with snow-covered cotton wool hills, mirrored skating rink lakes, houses, trees, moss, mushrooms and the like used to be very popular, but the tradition is not as widespread anymore.

CLAY

Flower, candle and spruce arrangements placed in clay, even with the addition of baubles and ribbons, are a well known way to decorate. They can be bought, but families with children do love to make them themselves. It is rather a popular tradition in many homes.

FLAWLESSLY AWESOME

METTE BECK ADSBØL

We pay a visit to Mette and her husband Mikkel, who built their dream home on a four-acre plot of land in North Zealand's countryside. Along with their two sons August and Karl, they live here in a 235 square metre whitewashed barn with a red tiled roof and delightful lake and forest views.

STYLIST, PRODUCT DESIGNER AND BOUTIQUE OWNER

Mette had 13 years of managerial experience at the renowned bakery chain Lagkagehuset, helping to expand the business throughout Denmark. An important factor for their success was designing the bakeries to be inviting, not least during the Christmas season. Mette found these responsibilities enjoyable and fulfilling, and this led her to establish herself as an independent product designer and interior stylist with her own boutique.

Her business concept is to encapsulate cosy, personal, unique and inviting ambiances in shops, cafes and restaurants. Mette became inspired to offer her clients custom-designed solutions and unique craftsmanship, after a few extended family trips to Morocco. She fell in love with the ancient, artisanal traditions and skills in this North African country, particularly in the manufacturing of wood, metal, carpets, textiles, glass and ceramics.

Mette and Mikkel's idea to live in the countryside came when they realised what a hassle it was for the family to do simple activities such as woodland walks. Why should it be so difficult? They felt that their children should grow up as they both had, with wide open spaces and fields. Mette's childhood was in southern Jutland and Mikkel grew up in central Zealand. The boys should learn to drive a tractor almost before learning how to ride a bike.

The family searched high and low for a house within a maximum driving distance radius of 45 minutes to Copenhagen, where they both worked at that time. After three years of hunting, they still could not find something with potential and on a beautiful natural plot. They came to the conclusion that they had to start building themselves. It certainly wasn't because the couple didn't try.

The reason their house resembles a barn, is because early on in the search process, the couple had found a plot with an existing old barn in a state of disrepair. So, Mette and Mikkel already had a detailed renovation and design plan on paper, down to the nearest detail. However, they ended up buying another plot. Now they had a plot and complete layout plans of a barn, but no actual barn! What could they do, but build one!

The impressive ceiling in the large open room is exceptionally high, and the over seven-metre-tall fireplace contributes as a bearing structure. This 100 square metre area contains a kitchen, dining area, living room and plenty of free floor space to romp about in. Most noticeable is the visible roof structure in the entire interior. And here, instead of using a plasterboard finish, a layer of bare planks is used. For the interior, Mette has prioritised wood, stone and Nordic hues, and she confidently combines Danish furniture classics together with Moroccan rugs and accessories.

It was in Morocco and especially Marrakech, where Mette encountered a range of skilled local artisans, in connection with sourcing unique interior products for her own décor. She quickly realised that should she be permitted to produce some of these items, there was good potential for a client base in Denmark, not just her own interior design projects.

"I love long-term solutions rather than what the current trend is. I choose with my heart and can quickly sense whether it is right or wrong. As a starting point, I always choose lasting and quality materials, becoming more beautiful over time, and preferably handmade. And I appreciate that sometimes it is worth spending a little more on a skilled carpenter or blacksmith to carry out unique work." METTE

"An old boyfriend's mother ran a cafe, and always said that food served to her customers should not just taste good, but look good. I have had this in mind ever since - even when I wrap presents. They should provide a feeling of hygge and warmth. I generally decorate with a twig, a fresh or dried flower or perhaps a bauble, pretty ribbon, and to top them off, one of my handmade brass stars. Should I have some pretty fabric remnants, I like to use some of it as a ribbon or extra decoration. I wrap gifts according to the motto - the joy of anticipation is the greatest." METTE

Mette's skill is also in understanding the adjustments required so that Moroccan products work in symbiosis with a Nordic interior style. It wasn't long before she had developed her own line of Berber rugs, ceramics and a wonderful and rustic collection of Christmas decorations.

When the family decorates for Christmas, they bring out old Christmas ornaments from Mette's grandparents and of course her brass and walnut stars with their gorgeous patina. The largest of them is 60 cm wide, and the smallest can sit in the palm of your hand. She had them made in collaboration with a carpenter and a blacksmith from a small town outside Marrakech. Each one is unique, hand crafted and subsequently sanded or beaten into shape. These stars will undoubtedly be passed down from generation to generation.

"As a child, my grandmother often took me around gorgeous boutiques, and this is where my fascination for quality products was born. My grandparents' home was full of hand-picked pieces from all over the world. Pieces that mattered to them. My grandfather was a carpenter, and his fine craftsmanship could easily stand up beside other good Danish designs. It was clear who lived in the house - and that is exactly what I always aspire to when I decorate - personal interior, for myself or for others." METTE

Mette and Mikkel always celebrate Christmas with their children's grandparents. They eat roast duck and a spicy rolled pork, white and browned potatoes and then Southern Jutland cabbage. The latter is a must if you, like Mette, are from this region. The only dish which has been allowed to sneak into the otherwise very traditional Southern Jutland Christmas dinner, is a fresh kale salad.

The Christmas meal is certainly enjoyed, but for the time being very much on the children's terms. Ris à l'amande is eaten, and when the little ones can wait no longer, they all dance and sing around the Christmas tree, then unwrap their presents. There is broad consensus that there shouldn't be a mad rush of gifts, where everyone gets hot and bothered, and ripped paper flies all over the place. Each present is unpacked, and appreciated and shown to each other.

Christmas and the traditional South Jutland cookies go hand in hand in this household. This specialty used to be more popular throughout Denmark, as mentioned before, but as with so many other old Danish recipes has been forgotten. It's certainly not forgotten in this household. Luckily, Mette is sharing her recipe with us.

MONSTERA
FLORA I
by ALL THE WAY TO PARIS
2014

"I made a conscious decision to apply bluer tones for our bedroom and bathroom walls. Blue hues are cool, yet fresh, and work well in our Nordic latitude too. Where art and Christmas decorations are concerned, they need not necessarily be reserved exclusively for the living room." METTE

WHITE MULLED WINE

GLÖGG

Serves 8

You will need:

2dl freshly squeezed orange juice

3 freshly squeezed lemons

2l quality apple juice

6 thin slices of ginger

6 anise stars

100g cane sugar

2 cinnamon sticks

1 quality vanilla pod

1dl white port wine

1dl light rum

Bring the orange, apple and lemon juice to the boil in a saucepan, along with the sugar and spices. Allow to simmer for 30 minutes.

Pour the mixture into a glass storage container with a lid, and allow it to sit for at least a day, if not up to a week.

Sieve the white glögg mix and bottle it.

To serve, warm it in a pan until it is a little below boiling point (2dl per glass serving). Add rum and port, just before serving, and decorate with star anise, or blanched almonds or sliced fresh ginger.

SOUTHERN JUTLAND COOKIES

SØNDERJYSKE FEDTKAGER

Medium portion

You will need:

250g organic pork lard

350g organic sugar

450g organic wheat flour

4tsp vanilla sugar

1tsp bicarbonate of soda

3tbsp cocoa (for the dark cookies)

Mix the pork lard and sugar together at room temperature. Combine the flour, vanilla sugar and bicarbonate of soda and knead it all together. Add cocoa to half of the dough.

Roll out to small balls and press them slightly flat. Bake for about 15 minutes at 165°C.

GIFTS

Gift giving was also a custom during the Viking era winter solstice festivities and early church Christmas celebrations. On the 28th December, children were celebrated in memory of the children slain in Bethlehem.

During the 13th century, these celebrations were moved to the 6th December, which is Saint Nicholas day. He was, as you recall, the patron saint of children. In honour of this day, children would receive a "Nicholas coin", which can be recorded as the very first Christmas gifts. This explains why Nicholas has become the official Christmas gift giver.

As far back as the Middle Ages, presents were first and foremost for children, and initially only really if they did well at school. If not, they were given rice. Until the 1700-1800s, more often than not, sacks of Christmas treats were given like ginger nuts, pastries such as klejner, and æbleskiver. Later on, came offerings of money and token gifts such as balls, jack in a boxes, cards and dolls.

But gifts could certainly be in the form of a much-needed item of clothing or a pair of shoes. They would often be homemade by a member of the family. Christmas has thus always been associated with generosity, including spreading joy by paying attention to the needy, as well as animals. Needless to say, elves too were served a bowl of rice pudding and a cup of ale.

GRATUITIES

Gifts for strangers, by way of gifts for workers also existed way back in the 1600 -1700s. Farmhands and servants often received a sack of foodwares of produce or treats, as thanks for their efforts and hard work with harvest, slaughtering animals and preparing for winter storage. One could receive fabric for new clothes, or simply cash gifts as a token of thanks. In fact, the word gratuity or gratitude stems from "gratia", meaning thanks.

The exchange of gifts between customers, suppliers and working partners comes from a time when the pastor, dean, blacksmith and others from the local area received dues by way of a gift at Christmas. Gratuities could also be an agreed part of the wages one was entitled to. Such gifts were almost a landlord's duty, and it was expected from nobility to their servants, or even kings to their subordinates.

SURPRISE GIFTS

Apart from these types of gratuities and treats, Christmas did not really imply large gift giving until the early 1800s.

In fact, priests were opposed to pampering, as they felt that Christmas was a time to reflect and worship. Exchanging surprise gifts began in the early 19th century. This was around the time that Christmas was for all people, and the Christmas tree came on the scene. Here, adults begin to give each other gifts as well. The presents were hung on the Christmas tree or laid out on a table or placed under the tree. To make it all the more exciting and surprising, during the 19th century, they began wrapping the presents and attaching a small gift verse to them, hinting of the contents to their recipient.

Children giving their parents small gifts they have made or bought with their own pocket money is no more than a 70-80-year-old tradition. In Scandinavia, gifts have always been given on Christmas Eve. It has to be said today, that the most exciting thing about Christmas for children is probably all the presents.

WRAPPING

It was not until the 20th century that Christmas gifts were wrapped and placed under the Christmas tree. Gift wrapping paper came about in the late 1800s. Originally it was white, glossy paper, then came strong colour print patterns on glossy or matte white paper. It has now become fashionable to make a huge effort with gift wrapping, and for some people a beautiful package is at least as important as the content. There is also clearly a certain status in gift wrapping from certain boutiques or department stores.

PAPER POETRY

AMANDA BETZ

Amanda bids us welcome into her lovely apartment in the middle of Frederiksberg. Christmas is in less than a week, and this year they are holding it here at home. She, her husband the music producer Fridolin and their two sons Charlie and Eddie will be celebrating juleaften in this gorgeous property, along with Fridolin's family, and Amanda's sister, brother-in-law, and their little boy.

ARCHITECT, DESIGNER AND PAPER ARTIST

Amanda comes from a family that has been through many divorces, which explains how highly she values creating and maintaining Christmas traditions to pass on to her own sons. She loves Christmas, the intimacy of yearly family Christmases and they are 100% on their children's terms.

One of these set family traditions takes place on the last Friday before Christmas. This involves chocolate making, and paper decorating. Amanda gathers the boys and a few of their friends together. Cutting paper is most certainly a skill Amanda has at her fingertips - if only we could master a few of them!

Amanda is an architect graduate from the Academy of Fine Arts' architecture school in Copenhagen. Her final thesis project was, in her own words, rather avant-garde. Nevertheless, it won first place, and Amanda was the recipient of the prestigious and coveted VOLA award.

It didn't take long for Amanda to realise that she was far too detail-oriented to work as a building architect, and so she moved quickly towards design. Fascinated by light and the filtering of artificial lighting, she designed lamps using paper, metal and wood. One of her assignments was for the well-known Danish lamp manufacturer Le Klint. A noticeable thread running through Amanda's lamp creations involves the refraction of light through cuts, or perforations in the material.

Amanda realised she really mastered moving from a two-dimensional to three-dimensional level, and very interesting and beautiful design details emerge with transformation of materials between these dimensions.

Today, Amanda works at the intersection of design and art, primarily with paper. She applies folding techniques according to legendary Japanese origami methods, and state of the art computer technology drawing methods and then cuts using machines. The work can varyingly be larger and smaller framed art structures. Sometimes they are commissioned works, displayed at art exhibitions or sold in galleries.

Amanda also works with handicraft projects. She's on the verge of launching a collection of utterly fairytale-like Christmas paper art. They are flat packed pieces such as cones, foliage and flowers, or small houses, that can be gently opened out into gorgeous three-dimensional decorations. Amanda is also behind the elegant Star Sun creation (as in the song "Lovely is the Blue Sky") that can hang from thin threads in windows or adorn the top of the Christmas tree. Perhaps it's unnecessary to mention the fact that Amanda has made all the decorations in her own home.

"Paper is a natural material like wood and glass. It comes from pulp and you can do anything with it. It can be shaped, cut, dissolved and renewed. It is like a blank canvas. It is the document that holds poetry. It is both fragile and strong." AMANDA

The Great Japan Exhibition
Art of the Edo Period 1600–1868

"Applying my knowledge as an architect, I have learned to transform and create ideas in my head to a two-dimensional drawing and then to a three-dimensional construction. The entire transformation can be contained in the paper. I can draw on it, fold and cut it up again. You can shape everything out of one piece." AMANDA

As Christmas Eve will be held at home, and the dining table in the kitchen is laid with Royal Copenhagen's beautiful white porcelain, and ornamental paper napkin rings - of course. The whole effect is a blend of muted pale whites and greens. Even the candles are slim and delicate. The top of the dining table has been designed by Amanda, and was made by the Copenhagen furniture carpentry firm Københavns Møbelsnedkeri.

Although Amanda has great respect for the artisan skill involved in cutting paper by hand, she does not see that there is anything wrong with using modern technology such as drawing programmes and laser cutters. Especially if that is what it takes to get the required result, namely ultra-fine and millimetre-precision cuts. The machines are able to do something even the most talented craftsman cannot, so why not?

As a general rule, Amanda's expressive style is extremely sophisticated and delicate. Much the same can be said about the decor of the almost 200 square metre apartment. The living room walls are painted in the palest delicate blush pink, and an elegant grey-blue velour sofa sits in the space. There are incredib e paper montages, lamps with folded paper shades, and baskets of paper. The work room blends in a really lovely way. There is paper everywhere - even tiny remnants lying nonchalantly on the floor in several places, an indication of creative expression and activity.

The favourite spot in the apartment is undoubtedly the built-in daybed in the bay window. It has been designed to store the necessarily huge amounts of paper in drawers under the mattress. A much-needed convenience when working from home. The daybed will also be a much-needed convenience on Christmas Eve, so that some family members can rest their full stomachs after the Christmas dinner is served in the kitchen.

"Paper flowers are created from the same principle as paper lace valentines' letters of old. Choose some pretty paper and ensure that it is a quadrangle (square), for example 15x15 cm. First fold towards the middle one way and then the other way. Hold on to the folded join, then snip and cut an identical leaf pattern at each corner. First, cut down from one side and then flip the paper down and cut an identical cut from the other side. Open up the paper and straighten the sheet. Now repeat with a new sheet of paper and cut another pattern. Lay the sheets on top of each other. As many as you like. Finally, tighten the layered flower together to a small stem at the base and fasten with tape or string. I have mounted my flower onto a bouquet of spruce and hung it to our front door." AMANDA

GOLD-DUSTED CONFECTIONERY

You will need:

Dark chocolate

Nougat

Marzipan

Dried mango slices

Fresh cranberries

Almonds

Gold and raspberry dust

Candied violets

Melt the chocolate and blanch the almonds. Slice the marzipan into delicate triangles. Layer them like small sandwiches, and decorate with the almonds, fresh cranberries (which although pretty, can be quite bitter) and candied violets. Dribble some of the dried fruit in melted chocolate, then decorate with gold and raspberry dust.

TREES

The Christmas tree tradition as we know it today is a culmination of several different cultural customs where trees have been featured. In Nordic mythology for example, the tree of life "Yaggdrasil" was an ash tree.

The first fir trees used in a Christmas context can be traced all the way back to ancient Livonia (Latvia and Estonia). It was here in 1441, where the first Christmas trees were erected in the two trade cities of Riga and Reval (Tallinn). However, the first decorated Christmas tree is believed to have first appeared in 1510 in Riga. In 2010, a plaque was laid in the central square of the city in commemoration of the 500th anniversary of the Christmas tree's origin

THE FIRST TREES IN DENMARK

In Denmark, the Christmas tree tradition started with Danish-German families introducing them to their own family Christmases. In 1808, Countess Wilhelmine Holstein from the South Zealand estate Holsteinborg lit the candles on possibly the first Christmas tree in Denmark.

The Christmas tree was introduced to Copenhagen in 1811 by the Lehmann family in Ny Kongensgade. It aroused great interest. Martin Gotlieb Lehmann was born in 1775, and was a priest's son from Haselau in Holsten, so he undoubtedly had Christmas trees at home as a child.
Martin Lehmann married Frederikke Louise Bech, a mayor's daughter in Copenhagen. In 1810 they had a son. They did not have a Christmas tree for their first Christmas in Ny Kongensgade together with little Orla. The following year the little family's father decided that they should, as he was used to in the rectory in Holsten, where he grew up. One of the guests who visited the family that Christmas Eve wrote about the excitement it aroused amongst townsfolk.

"Each and every room facing the street was illuminated, and at 5'o'clock on Christmas Eve, there were many curious passersby stopping under the windows in wonder and amazement. The rumour had spread in the neighbourhood that a wonderful tall fir tree had been brought into the living room in Ny Kongensgade a few days before, and that it would be candlelit. Everyone peeled their eyes to catch a glimpse. The first Christmas tree in Copenhagen could not be missed. Some of us thought the young doctor and his lovely wife had gone crazy since they had drawn back their curtains and attached live candles to a fir tree."

THE CUSTOM

This Christmas tree custom spread quite slowly in Copenhagen, and was really still regarded as only a German tradition for the first half a dozen years. It wasn't until just before World War I that it became more common in Danish homes. It was about the same time (1914) when the newspaper Politiken lit the first outdoor Christmas tree in Denmark, at Copenhagen's Town Hall Square.

Over the course of 150 years, Scandinavian Christmas tradition has included a tree. After all, it is the undisputed centerpiece of festive celebrations in almost every home - at least one with children in it. For many it's no longer about whether to have a Christmas tree, but more about how big and what kind. There is a variety to choose from.

NORDMANN SPRUCE

This fir tree is characterized by not having prickly needles and having a long shelf life after harvest - especially if the tree is placed in water. The trunk bark is completely smooth and grey. The upper side of the needles are dark green and glossy and the underside has two blue-white stripes.

Generally, this Nordmann spruce has good needles and branches, and tends to be the preferred Christmas tree species in many places in Europe because of its appearance and good durability. Over the past 15 years, demand for it has overtaken many original Christmas tree species such as red spruce, blue spruce and various pine species.

RED SPRUCE

Needles on the red spruce are only 1-2 cm long, green and prickly. They also shed more easily than Nobilis and Nordmann spruce. If you cut them, they have a square cross section, and each outer side has a bright stripe. The bark is reddish brown on the young trees and on the branches, and the trunk has small scales. With age, the bark becomes more greyish brown and the scales become larger and coarser.

The red spruce is still considered to be the "original" Christmas tree in Nordic countries. Since central heating became commonplace, the indoor climate has become warmer and drier. Unfortunately, the red spruce dries out faster now than in the old days, which often leads to more extensive needle shedding. This can however be significantly reduced if the tree is placed in water, to avoid drying out. Evaporation can also be limited if the tree is brought inside at the last minute. This can test the patience of any small child!

NOBILIS

The Nobilis, or as it is often called in Danish, silver spruce, has soft almost silvery needles - a mixture between blue-grey and teal. They are about 3 cm long, tightly packed, and look the same above and below. For this reason, shoots and branches look very attractive. The bark on a Nobilis is smooth, pale grey and filled with resin blisters, and not dissimilar to elephant skin. Nobilis is one of the Christmas tree species with the best shelf life after harvest, which is also why Nobilis branches cuttings are used for Advent wreaths and Christmas decorations.

It is more difficult to grow quality Nobilis fir in a Danish climate, as fewer buds appear on branches than on the Nordmann spruce. It can also be prone to bud death, further reducing the number of branches, so resulting in a lack of symmetry.

POT GROWN TREES

Lately, a number of Danish companies such as Danmarks Skove (Denmark's forests), offer sustainable Christmas trees. These trees are pot grown so can be recycled rather than felled. When the tree has outgrown its pot and can no longer be traded, it is planted back into the forest.

Trees, including Christmas trees, absorb CO_2 from the air and bind it. When the trees perish either by decay or combustion, most of the CO_2 absorbed is released. If the tree remains standing therefore, it can absorb large amounts of CO_2 and ensure that we have a better climate in the future.

The idea of pot-grown recycled Christmas trees is a good one. However, there is a bigger picture. One must also consider the climate cost, in that fossil fuel is used when transporting trees back and forth.

COLOUR COURAGE

NADIA LASSEN

Nadia Lassen, her boyfriend Kasper and the couple's four small daughters - Aya, Norma, Alva and Flora look forward to a calmer Christmas than they have had in years. Here, on a residential road in Frederiksberg, a long and protracted renovation is finally over, and they can enjoy their home.

DESIGNER AND SERIAL ENTREPRENEUR

The redevelopment of this large house was extensive. It required both exterior and interior renovation, plus a new terrace and garden were also to be established. Luckily, Nadia's experience with this level of work was very current. She had renovated another house in the neighborhood just a few years back.

For most people, this in itself would have been a full-time job. In 2008 however, Nadia, who is Mogens Lassen's great granddaughter, established the By Lassen design company, along with her uncle and her partner Peter Østerberg. It has had tremendous success in relaunching classic designs, the most well-known being the Cube, a square candlestick with four candles that every Danish design lover has standing in their home. In a short time space, sales of this iconic piece rocketed.

By Lassen also secured the rights to the production of Flemming Lassen's furniture. In 1935, Flemming, who was Mogens' brother, had designed an extremely inviting armchair, upholstered in lambskin, for The Copenhagen Cabinetmakers' Guild Competition. This characteristic teddy bear shaped chair attracted as much attention then as it does today. In Flemming Lassen's own words, sitting in this chair should feel "as warm and safe as a polar bear cub feels in his mother's arms in the middle of the ice cap". The chair was named The Tired Man. In 2015, an early version of the armchair reached a staggering hammer price of DKK 1.42 million at Bruun Rasmussen auction house. It became the most expensive design chair in Denmark to date. By Lassen was right to predict the potential in relaunching this icon.

A few years ago, Nadia sold her share of By Lassen to her uncle. Now that she had a taste for entrepreneurship, and had proven her knack for it, she felt compelled to try something new. In 2016, with Peter Østerberg as a partner again, she launched the lighting company Nuura. Lighting designer Sofie Refer came on board. Within a very short time frame, Nuura - Norse for light and honour - has established an exclusive dealer network and launched an extensive collection - with a chandelier as the focal point for each product line. Nadia is also a partner in the Danish design company Gejst.

So everyday life for Nadia is understandably busy. In broad contrast to that, Christmas is devoted to family. Nadia equates Christmas with closeness, love, a time for reflection and looking back at the past year. Her childhood Christmases were with her grandparents in their country house in Odsherred. She recalls with fondness visiting her grandparents as soon as she was on Christmas break, and staying there all Christmas, every year. Christmas Eve itself was brimming with tradition and her extended family would gather around the table. Cousins, uncles and aunts, siblings and her parents. The tradition of holding Christmas at her grandparents was such an ingrained part of her childhood that Nadia never actually held Christmas in her own childhood home.

"Put bluntly, Christmas isn't quite Christmas without a tree at home! So much tradition centres around the Christmas tree, and I have vivid recollections of my own childhood when we decorated the Christmas tree together on the 23rd December." NADIA

"We didn't have a traditional four-candle Advent wreath when I grew up. Instead of lighting candles one by one every Sunday, we had an arrangement, prettily decorated with ribbon and spruce, with all four candles lit simultaneously. I have continued this custom, so have never actually had a traditional Advent wreath, though I do light the candles every Sunday. This year I made our Advent decoration using a large marble dish. I filled the base with moss, and placed four shiny chrome candlesticks in it. Being modular, the candlesticks can be shaped to your liking. Four lacquered delicate purple handmade candles finish the look well, with their extra length and beautiful conical form. A true Advent Sunday ambiance." NADIA

Now that Nadia's grandmother is no longer alive, Nadia has established her own traditions for the family and their four little girls. One of which is the stockings hanging in the kitchen - one for each child - that get filled with a small gift each December morning. Another is baking diligently throughout the festive season - gingernuts, butter cookies and ginger biscuits. They do this very thing every weekend throughout the Christmas month. And then of course the delightfully ornamental Christmas tree, with its flag garlands, different coloured candles, and a wonderful mix of new and vintage baubles, hearts and figures. A great deal is homemade - created by children and adults alike. Every year, Nadia also buys a new ornament for the collection. This year's new addition is a charming little Tivoli carousel. After all, Nadia and Kasper met in Tivoli Gardens.

"Our tree is allowed to come indoors early in December, because I love to see it stand and sparkle in the living room. We still decorate it together, using traditions passed down from my family. Each year we make new ornaments, writing our name and the year, and save them year after year. My oldest daughter loves to see the decorations she made when she was very little. I relish in the fact that nothing is perfect, and that the Christmas tree reflects a celebration of family and hearts." NADIA

Nadia's confidence is not only evident in the business world, but also in a personal setting. The selection of the deep red colour chosen for their kitchen elements and the beautiful large-floral bathroom wallpaper clearly prove that she is surely not afraid of colour or pattern. It is so atmospheric.

GLUTEN-FREE VANILLA COOKIES

VANILJEKRANSE

You will need:

1 vanilla pod

250g soft butter

250g caster sugar

1 egg

125g potato flour

100g whole grain rice flour

125g rice flour

75g buckwheat flour

Split the vanilla pods lengthways and scrape the seeds out with a knife. Mix with a little sugar to spread them. Mix the soft butter, sugar and vanilla together using a hand mixer, then add the rest of the ingredients.

Work the dough into a ball, then refrigerate, preferably until the following day, but at least a couple of hours. It is very important that the dough is cold, so that it can be formed and keep its shape.

When making the vanilla cookie dough shapes, there are several options. The nicest and easiest is to run the dough through a star shaped chopper. Alternatively, you can simply roll the dough into small sausages, curl them into rings and press the ends together.

The vanilla wreaths are baked at 180 °C convection oven, for approximately. 8 minutes. They should be pale brown at the edge but not too dark.

Let the vanilla cookies cool on the baking tray. Gluten-free cookies are more porous than regular ones, so they break easily if you move them before they've cooled. Once cooled, they are a little more stable.

The vanilla cookies can be kept in a biscuit tin at room temperature for a long time, so you can definitely bake them well before Christmas. Naturally, their taste and texture quality decreases over time, but do not hesitate to bake them 3-4 weeks before Christmas.

Tip: You can easily freeze half of the dough, so that you can bake another batch later.

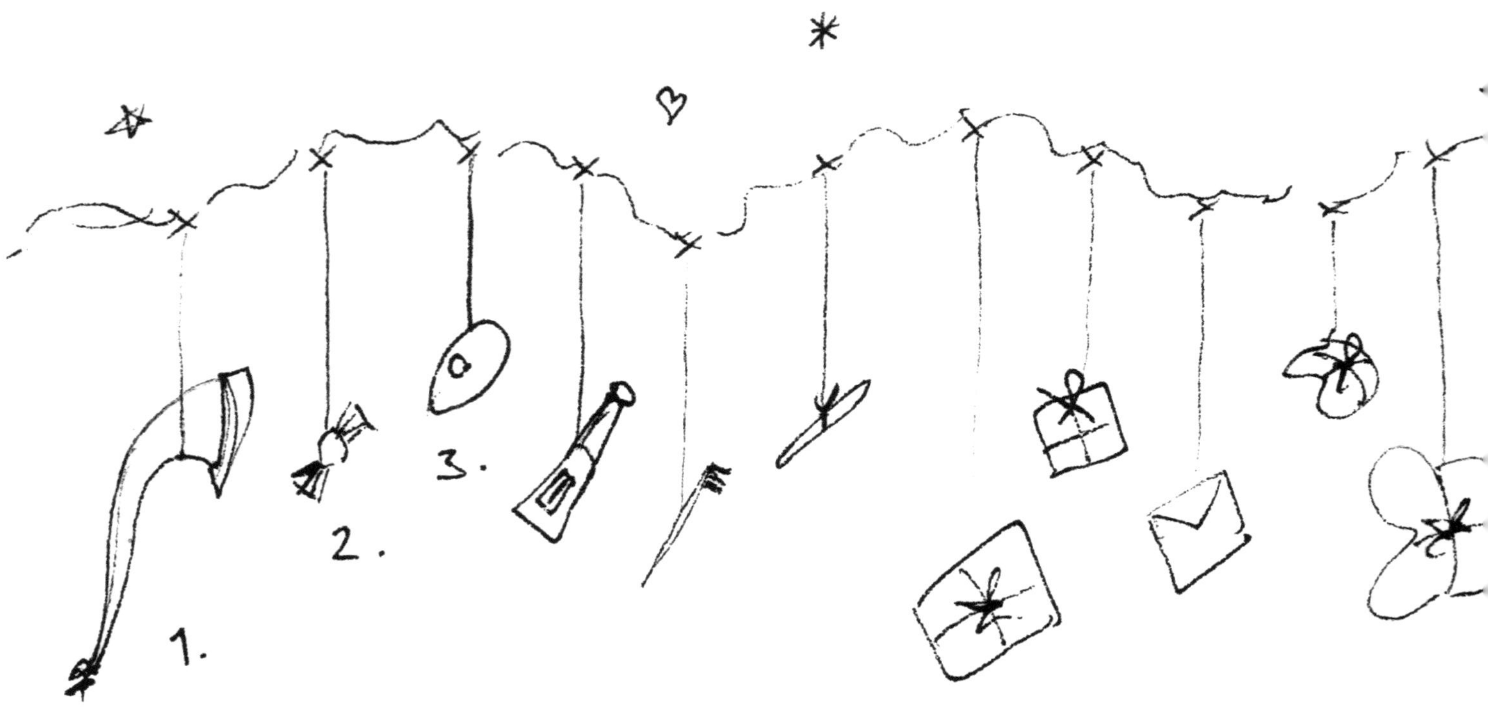
1.
2.
3.

24
23.

CALENDARS

The Christmas gift calendar tradition is not a Scandinavian but a German concept, introduced to children in Denmark in 1932. The Germans and the English have flat Christmas calendars with doors numbered for every day in December. These Advent calendars are even older.

The Christmas calendar story begins from early last century, when the Bavarian publisher Gerhard Lang invented this charming and much-loved Christmas tradition. It consisted of two sheets of card. One had biblical verses or proverbs, and another had images of angels. The idea was you'd read the verse, and then glue the corresponding image onto it.

It is said that it was his mother who first laid the foundation for this popular new custom, in order to while away the days before little Gerhard could celebrate Jesus' birth. His mother packed treats and goodies into small daily December packages, which were unwrapped with joy and great enthusiasm. Something to nibble on until Christmas Eve was upon them.

Later on, in Munich, Gerhard Lang thought up the concept of designing doors on the first sheet, which was glued on top of the second, so a sort of picture book effect was achieved. By the 1920s, Gerhard Lang's Advent calendars slowly but surely began to win the hearts of excited children (and their families) all over the world.

Over in Denmark, the art publishers Chr. Olsens introduced this German concept, producing the first Advent calendar in 1932. At the same time, English cardboard Christmas calendars were being published, but without ribbons and decorations. Instead, there were images of Santa Claus, drums, rocking horses, Christmas trees and other festive symbols.

The trend really caught on. Even before World War II, children in Denmark could play with the three-dimensional Christmas calendars, where you would find goodies like elves, trains and planes.

GIFT CALENDARS

After World War II, the Christmas package calendar became rather popular. Back then however, they tended to be homemade. People would make or buy fabric Christmas calendars to be hung on walls. They usually had 24 pockets in them which could hold gifts - large or small. Sometimes rings were sewn onto the fabric so presents could be tied to them. Businesses often market the sale of what's known as calendar gifts, for this very purpose.

Nowadays, many make personal package calendars for a loved one - whether their children, husband, wife, partners or parents. The joy in receiving such a personal present is indescribable.

CHRISTMAS CALENDARS ON TV

In 1962, Denmark's Radio's Children and Youth Department began producing a "Children's Christmas Calendar Show". This was initiated from Sweden, who had started a few years before. They started as daily radio broadcasts and later switched to the television medium. It was based on a countdown to Christmas, so was a 24-episode series airing from the 1st December to the 24th December, with a charitable Christmas theme.

Since 1977, Denmark's Radio renamed this tradition, so that it focused on underdeveloped countries, with the aim of raising awareness and funds towards children's projects in poorer countries. This worthwhile calendar is a collaboration between Denmark's Radio, DANIDA and other children's charities.

TV Christmas calendars are still incredibly popular (for children and adults) and there is virtually no TV station in Scandinavia that does not produce a Christmas calendar.

THE STOCKING

Since the 1900s, countless Christmas traditions have been introduced from the USA and Britain. No small example is the Christmas stocking, which is one of the most popular Christmas traditions in English speaking countries. On Christmas Eve, children hang a stocking beside the fireplace or at the foot of their bed. After all, Santa Claus needed a place to put his presents. That is, if you have behaved all year. If not, you risk getting a lump of charcoal. The children then excitedly make a dash to their stockings on Christmas morning.

There are a number of established traditions that must be observed. Santa Claus has a busy 24 hours, so you must ensure that you set things out to him for sustenance. He has a hearty appetite, and a bit of a sweet tooth. Do leave out a tray with something edible, and something to quench his thirst. He's partial to small gifts of some sort or other.

In fact, the Christmas stocking actually originated in Europe, around the middle ages when children started to receive gifts. The custom of hanging something up for the presents to be placed arrived in the 1300-1400s. Initially, it was Saint Nicholas who delivered presents. He was also the patron saint of sailors, so children in southern Germany would leave out model ships to fill. In other parts of Europe, including the Netherlands, clogs were used. They were later replaced by stockings, and Dutch emigrants brought the custom with them to the United States, where it became widespread in the 19th century.

In the past, a regular stocking was used, but eventually special homemade or bought Christmas stockings became a steadfast tradition. If you do not have the time before the 1st December to make a package calendar with all 24 gifts ready, an excellent alternative is putting a gift in a stocking every day.

FAIRYTALE FLAIR

VIOLISE LUNN

Violise Lunn has lived in her small apartment in a classic Copenhagen property close to the lakes for years. The furniture, primarily heirlooms and vintage finds, does rather fill the space. However, the overriding impression is of beautiful, fresh and light creative chaos.

DESIGNER AND PAPER ARTIST

The art on the walls are a blend of family pieces, or creations by friends and family. Her own mother, the visual artist Merete Zacho, is behind some of the larger pieces. A charming little box collage on the kitchen wall has the inscription ,"Villas are too close to the ground for Violise". A delightful personal gift from designer colleague and friend Louise Campbell.

There really isn't space for a standard Christmas tree. But there's nothing standard about Violise's solution. There is a lovely vase on the coffee table, which holds branches with dangling decorations that are just as atmospheric as an entire tree. In fact, the bare branches give the ornaments more visibility than had they been on a spruce tree. Most of them are made by Violise herself, and the rest are antique. Also created by Violise and available for sale in her studio, are the big stars in the window. The decadently charming white paper lamps adorning the space were made for a gallery exhibition for light objects.

Visiting Violise is like being invited behind the scenes at the Royal Theatre - such a sense of fantasy, creativity and buzz. Everything is going on at the same time. There is project planning for Christmas ornaments and piece samples for Violise's own "theatre scenery". So many different imaginative activities.

Violise's own workshop and sewing room in Gothersgade may be merely a ten-minute walk from the apartment, but she can't do without a work space and her tools at home. As soon as she gets an idea it must be tested, hence the scissors, paint, brush, glass, cardboard, tools and not least paper in all shades. They must be ready at hand.

A trained fashion designer from the Danish Design School, Violise has been independent since the late 1990s. She designs dresses - especially wedding dresses - for her clients, and also creates shoes and paper dresses. The latter is either for special exhibitions, or simply because she can't help it. The dresses are to die for, including those of paper. One could describe Violise's talents as being a fusion of art and design.

Hanging from the ceiling are divine paper tutus, made for the 2018 exhibition "Glass, Fashion and Fantasy" at the Hempel Glass Museum in Annebjerg near Nykøbing Sjælland. They are beautifully decorated with thin, crystal like and clear pieces of Muscovite (folklore calls them Maria glass). In the old days, Maria glass symbolised purity, so was often used on images of saints. The name muscovite comes from Muscovy-glass, used in Elizabethan England and medieval Russia as a cheaper alternative to glass in windows. Violise has loved the material since she found beautiful shards in the Swedish archipelago as a child, and she uses it diligently.

Creativity is not unheard of in Violise's family. One could say it was genetic. Handicrafts and artistry were the way they spent time together. Her mother had a large studio in the house annex, and there was ample to get your hands on, like yarn, paint and paper. Both her grandmothers sewed and embroidered. In fact, one grandmother's basement floor was knee high with layers of fabric residue from hours of creativity.

FIL D'IRLANDE
A LA CROIX
FIL SPÉCIAL

And it wasn't just the mother's side of the family. Violise and her sister built rabbit cages and playhouses with their creative father, and there is no doubt that this relaxed approach has led to Violise being so talented today. Put simply, she was encouraged to make things as a child. The sisters were given free reign to use everything and anything, and be inventive - within reason of course.

Violise's immersion in her family's nurturing and inspirational childhood, meant that her talents could be released, and she now produces a spectrum of practical or purely aesthetic pieces. However, she starts from the same point - allowing for imagination and the pursuit of perfection.

Christmas Eve was always a busy and large family affair in Violise's childhood, her parents held it with both sides of the family, cousins, and often more distant relatives. The rest of the Christmas holiday however, was calmer and spent with friends and cosy visits.

One thing was certain. Christmas Eve was certainly very traditional. Everyone was welcome and the Christmas dinner offered roast turkey, a glazed ham that Violise's Swedish grandmother always brought, and rice pudding was for dessert. After dinner, dancing around the Christmas tree, and opening Christmas presents, the evening always ended with a slideshow of the year that had passed.

Violise works with Christmas in a professional capacity, and so her small apartment has Christmas decorations all year round. She designs Christmas ornaments for commercial clients such as Royal Copenhagen, and also has a small collection of her own, which she sells privately and from her annual Christmas market. In addition, she is often commissioned to decorate shops for the festive season. Twice now, Violise has been given the honour of designing a Christmas table for Royal Copenhagen in their Amagertorv boutique showroom.

The perfectionist in her means that she experiments with ideas at home, so that when Christmas finally comes around, she is completely satisfied with the results. For a few years now, Violise has celebrated Christmas by travelling abroad with her boyfriend and friends. They can all relax, soak in another culture, and enjoy the local cuisine. An excellent substitute for the traditional gift fest and rich Danish Christmas meals. Besides, she can return to Denmark recharged, and with a renewed zest and inspiration for next year's Christmas creations.

"Making unwearable items from the simplest texture of all: paper, is one of my greatest passions. Finding perfect freedom in this material through sculpting figure silhouettes, angels and shoes, I allow myself to play with otherwise impossible compositions. The sheer lightness and utter fragility combined with experimental reflection about what these objects represent, fascinates me deeply." VIOLISE

"These angels here are simple to make yourself. I cut or tear two paper squares of 7x7 cm and a square of 12x12 cm. Glue them into two small cones, then glue them together afterwards, as the image shows. Allow them to dry. Glue the thread and hair on the head, and allow to dry. Then glue the head on the body and draw a small face." VIOLISE

WARM ORANGE WINE

You will need:

Sirup:

1kg organic oranges

1kg sugar

Water

When serving: Red wine

Cut whole oranges into quarters and place them in a large pot, filling with water until they are covered. Pour in the sugar and simmer for at least five hours without a lid until completely dark. When cooled, sieve so that the syrup is separated from the flesh (tasty as a chutney or orange marmalade).

To serve, mix about 2 cups of orange syrup with a bottle of red wine and warm up. Pour more wine in if it is too sweet or vice versa. Decorate with fresh orange slices.

Orange wine tastes a little fresher and lighter and is a good alternative to the slightly heavier and spicy glögg.

Tip: The red wine can be replaced with white wine and you can also add slices of fresh ginger to the syrup while it is boiling.

HEDGEHOG CONFECTIONERY

You will need:

Marzipan

Dates

Dark chocolate

Chopped hazelnuts

Optional: Candied violets and rum

Take a date and pit it, then slot an almond in. If the dates are large, then use half.

Roll out a piece of marzipan, placing the date in it, and form a small hedgehog snout. Dip the back end into melted dark chocolate and then straight into the chopped nuts. Make blue eyes of candied violets or cake decorations.

You can also drip a little rum onto the marzipan.

DRINKS

Festive beer drinking is a very old pagan custom. Ample quantities of beer were drunk during Viking solstice parties, and one could say that celebrating Christmas was a Drinking Christmas. A law in the 900s stipulated that Christmas should last as long as a barrel of beer lasted. The word beer meant party, and so Christmas beer also meant Christmas party.

BEER

When Christianity arrived, the church accepted this beer drinking culture to an extent. In fact, in the 11th century it was decided that Christmas beer drinking should always begin with a toast in Jesus Christ's name. This custom continued well into the 19th century.

Danes would usually start the brewing process shortly before the Christmas season, and Thomas Day (the 21st December) was often the big brewing day. Compared to everyday beer, Christmas beer called "Santa Claus" was produced with extra malt and honey, which made it both stronger and sweeter.

CHRISTMAS WHITE BEER

Out in the countryside, people continued to brew their own beer at home, but in townships, breweries sold especially fermented and extra sweet white beer for Christmas. Christmas white beer was the typical Christmas beer for many years, including the introduction of the popular "Nisse beer" from Kongens Bryghus in the 1890s.

Christmas or Santa's beer is alcohol-lite white beer, so very suitable for the young and other young at hearts, here around Christmas time. Hints of dark malt, bread, prunes, dark brown sugar, caramel and maybe even a touch of licorice can be traced in this white beer. The dessert-like taste is a lovely accompaniment with rice pudding, cinnamon sugar and butter, but is also super with ris à l'amande.

CHRISTMAS ALE

The Danes' strong Christmas brew first came in earnest in the 1960s. It was Albani who launched the first, but other breweries soon followed suit. Today, the launch of the annual Christmas beer is a major marketing event, not least with Tuborg's "Snow Beer", around since 1981 and always released on a special "J-Day" with special events and promotions. Since 1999, J-Day has taken place on the first Friday in November.

SNAPS AND WINE

It became contagious. The tradition of drinking beer and festivities soon led to other beverages joining the party! This is especially true of snaps; a faithful guest at Christmas lunch tables around Denmark and Scandinavia as a whole.

On the 24th December, wine became the more usual drink to accompany Christmas Eve dinner. Once reserved for nobility, it spread to the bourgeoisie in the 19th century. Many wine lovers ponder their Christmas wine choice. Roast duck, which most of us Danes swear by as our traditional dish, has both an intense and strong flavour. However, it is also very rich, which one should bear in mind when selecting Christmas wine. Remember to think of the side dishes too, as duck gravy is rich, red cabbage is sour, and caramelised potatoes are sweet. Rather a tall order for choosing the right wine. I do not claim to be a connoisseur, but many people like to discuss the choices diligently.

MULLED WINE

Glögg comes from the word "glödgad" literally meaning burned. It originated as a form of warm toddy and was most popular in the bourgeois community of the 1800s.

Glögg originated in Sweden and was introduced to Danish Christmas celebrations in the 1940s, together with a number of other Swedish Christmas traditions. Mulled wine or spirits are burnt in sugar and added to raisins, almonds and spices. In fact, glögg was not a definitive Christmas drink in Sweden at all. It was simply one of the many toddies so popular in the 19th century. It wasn't until about 1900 that it became associated with Christmas, because the warm, sweet beverage was so suited for the chilly mid-winter.

There are actually two main types of mulled drink: wine glögg and spirit glögg. Their names speak for themselves. Wine glögg has a wine base, and has a history stemming from warm, spicy wines of antiquity. It is of the same genre as other "Glühwein" from Austria and Switzerland. Spirit glögg is based on spirits and is inspired by the French "brulôt" - warm cognac and sugar that came to the Nordic countries in the 1600s.

Today one can buy ready-made red and white mulled wine, or semi-finished products where you just have to add wine, almonds and raisins. Many however, still enjoy making their own version.

Glögg tastes great and is a charmingly atmospheric festive drink tradition. The smell and taste of the sweet yet spicy alcohol fills you with a glow, from your head to your toes, keeping out the cold from the snow and frost. Just what is needed after a search in the plantation for your perfect Christmas tree. Another sign that it's not long to go before Christmas Eve, and a really merry Christmas is upon you.

INFORMATION

In the following pages, you can find contact details of the people you have met throughout the book, and information about products shown in the twelve homes we have visited. I have focused on products and designs on the market. The vintage, heirlooms, flea market finds, unique pieces, art and quriosa are only mentioned if we know where they can be sourced from. I have endeavoured to organise the list to follow the same order as the images are in the book.

PRODUCTS

MONOCHROME MOODS

Outside: Pot grown red spruce, via Denmark's Forests. **Hall:** Coat Rack Bench, designed by Front, produced by Thonet Vienna. Adnet mirror, designed by Jacques Adnet, produced by Gubi. Vintage Radiohus pendant, designed by Wilhelm Lauritzen, produced by Louis Poulsen. Wall colour, Railings, produced by Farrow & Ball. **Kitchen:** Kitchen elements, designed and produced by Henrik Falk. Wall colour, Strong White, produced by Farrow & Ball. Vintage chopping boards, via Fil de Fer and K&Co. Round chopping board, produced by Eva Solo. Round trays, designed and produced by Woud and Iben Bach Studio. Wooden star, designed by and distributed via Mette Beck Adsbøl. **Dining room:** SE68 chairs, designed by Egon Eiermann, produced by Wielde und Spieth. Vintage pendant, designed by Poul Henningsen, produced by Louis Poulsen. Oil painting by Kehnet Nielsen, via Gallery Susanne Ottesen. Sculptures by Josefine Winding and Noa Gammelgaard. Table lamp, designed and produced by Klassik Studio. Curtains, in fabric from C&C Milan, produced by Tapet-Café. Wall colours, Pigeon and Strong White, produced by Farrow & Ball. Vintage Longton Hall dinnerware, produced by Mulberry Home. Focus de Luxe cutlery, produced by Gense. Nagel candlesticks, produced by Stoff Copenhagen. Napkins, produced by Linum. Tablecloth, produced by Hør Her. Unique ceramic jar, created by Cathrine Raben Davidsen. Contour vase, designed by Turi Heisselberg Pedersen, produced by Kahler Design. Tray, designed and produced by Nordal Interiors. Duca candlestick, designed by Krøyer-Sætter-Lassen, produced by Menu. Blossi table lamp, designed by Sofie Refer, produced by Nuura. Oil painting by Preben Hornung, via Bruun Rasmussen. **Living room:** Tokyo sofa, designed by Niels Gammelgaard, produced by SITS Furniture. Vintage office chair, designed by Arne Jacobsen, produced by Fritz Hansen. Wassily lounge chairs, designed by Marcel Breuer, produced by Knoll Studio. Vintage floor and ceiling lamps, designed by Jean-Louis Domecq, produced by Jieldé. Storage system, designed by Jakob Wagner, produced by Montana Furniture Vintage cabinet, via Fil de Fer. Oil paintings by Jens Brok and Anne Tholstrup. Art by Sophie Klerk and Line Busch. Sculptures by Josefine Winding and Tilde Grynnerup. Vase, designed and produced by Nordal Interiors. Objects, designed and produced by Klassik Studio. Paper basket, produced by Lillerød. Mobile, created by Kasper Friis Kjeldgaard. The Frame TV, produced by Samsung. Wall clock and ring, produced by Menu. Curtains, in fabric from C&C Milan, produced by Tapet-Café. Vintage Beni Ourain rugs. Wall colour, Strong White, produced by Farrow & Ball. **Bedroom:** Pendel designed by Poul Henningsen, produced by Louis Poulsen. Vintage table, produced by Mulberry Home. Vintage side shell chair, designed by Ray & Charles Eames, produced by Herman Miller. Table lamps, designed and produced by Klassik Studio. Bedcover, in fabric from Andrew Martin, produced by Tapet-Café. Curtains, in fabric from C&C Milan, produced by Tapet-Café. Wall colour, Light Blue, produced by Farrow & Ball. Bedside table, designed by New Works.

FLOWER POWER

Living room: Daybed, designed by Ole Gjerløv-Knudsen, produced by Skovshoved Møbelsnedkeri. Spring mattress, produced by IKEA. Pillows, produced by Marimekko. Pillows, designed and made by Leif Sigersen. Vintage wall clock, via flea market in Sweden. Vintage paintings, via flea market in Sweden. Lounge chairs, via Helsingborgs Antique fair. Vintage office chair, via flea market in Denmark. Vintage shelves, via flea market in New York. Vintage rugs, via flea market in Sweden. **Kitchen:** The Ant dining chair, designed by Arne Jacobsen, produced by Fritz Hansen. Conch dinnerware, designed by Arje Griegst, produced by Royal Copenhagen. Ruska stoneware, designed by Ulla Procopé, produced by Arabia. Egeløv glass, produced by Holmegaard. Silver cutlery, designed by Sigvard Bernadotte and Arne Jacobsen, produced by Georg Jensen. Vase, designed by and distributed via Leif Sigersen.

COSY COUNTRY

Hall: Art, by Cathrine Borge. Arctic Pear chandelier, designed and produced by Ochre. **Living room:** Sofa, designed by Paola Navone, produced by Gervasoni. Lounge chair, designed by Ray og Charles Eames, produced by Herman Miller. Ari lounge chair, designed by Ari Norell, produced by Norell Furniture. Console, designed and produced by House Doctor. Art by Kristine Vintervold, Cathrine Borge and F1. Rug, designed and produced by Massimo. Table lamp, designed by Jean-Louis Domecq, produced by Jieldé. Wall lamp, designed and produced by José Esteves. **Dining room:** Catch chairs, designed by Jamie Hayon, produced by &Tradition. Tablecloth, produced by Linge Particulier. Perfect Imperfection dinnerware, designed by Roos van de Velde, produced by Serax. Bine cutlery, produced by House Doctor. **Kitchen:** Tolix chairs, designed by Xavier Pauchard, produced by Tolix. Ceiling lamp, designed by José Esteves. Tablecloth, produced by Society. Chopping board, designed and produced by Raumgestalt.

SIMPLY SCULPTURAL

Dining room: Tulip dining table, designed by Eero Saarinen, produced by Knoll. Serving tray, designed by Camilla Rosén, produced by C/RO. Kulan candlestick, designed by Estrid Ericson, produced by Svenskt Tenn. Vintage Bauhaus chairs. Vintage mirror, found at Fil de Fer. eWall lamp, designed by Les Corbusier, produced by Ambiente. **Living room:** Gift boxes, produced by Karl Lund Papir. Filip sofa, designed and produced by Ihreborn. Coffee table, designed and produced by Hay. Rug, designed and produced by Massimo. Ceiling lamp, designed by Woltec, via C/RO. Macaron side table (prototype), designed by Camilla Rosén, produced by C/RO. Sebastian chair, designed by Camilla Rosén, produced by C/RO. Vase, designed and produced by Skrufs Glasbruk. Marble tray, designed and produced by Hay. Table lamp, designed and produced by Flos. The Doodle sculpture, created by Sofia Tufvasson. **Bedroom:** Bed, designed and produced by IKEA. Bedlinen, designed and produced by HM Home. Snoopy table lamp, designed by Castiglioni, produced by Flos. **Hall:** Bench, designed and produced by Bolia. **Kitchen:** Bar stool, designed and produced by IKEA. Dagg vase, designed by Carina Seth Andersson, produced by Svenskt Tenn. Vintage Edged Blue Flower tea cups and saucers, designed by Arnold Krog, produced by Royal Copenhagen.

ECLECTIC OPULENCE

Living room: Jules sofa, designed and produced by George Smith. Etagere, designed and produced by Vaughan. Coffee table, designed and produced by Donghia for Rubelli. Lounge chairs, designed by Vaughan, upholstered in Dedar fabric via Tapet-Café. Rug, designed and produced by Christopher Farr. Lamps, designed and produced by Vaughan. PK54 dining table, designed by Poul Kjærholm, produced by Fritz Hansen. Danish vintage chairs, upholstered in fabric from Pierre Frey, via Tapet-Café. Vintage cocktail cabinet, designed by Klaus Wettergren. Curtains, in Como Collection, designed by Helene Blanche, produced by Tapet-Café. Oil painting by Tal R, via Gallery Bo Bjerggaard. Art by Asger Mortensen and Damien Hirst. Mobile by Kirstine Roepstorff. Sculptures from A-Kassen, via Gallery Nicolai Wallner. Wall colours, India Yellow and Railings, produced by Farrow & Ball. **Dining room:** CH33 chairs, designed by Hans J. Wegner, produced by Carl Hansen. Ceiling pendant, designed and produced by Vaughan. Table lamp, designed and produced by Collier-Webb. Tablecloth, fabric from Dedar, via Tapet-Café. Dinnerware, designed by Ponti produced by Richard Ginori. Curtains, in Como Collection, designed by Helene Blanche, produced by Tapet-Café. Wall colour, Down Pipe, produced by Farrow & Ball. **Kitchen:** Kitchen elements, designed and produced by Kvänum, painted in Hardwick White from Farrow & Ball. Collage by Tal R, via Gallery Bo Bjerggaard. Oil painting by Alexander Tovborg, via Gallery Nicolai Wallner. Wall colour, Hardwick White, produced by Farrow & Ball. **Bathroom:** Sanitation and fixtures, designed by Volewatch, via Aquadoma. Wall colour, Hardwick White, produced by Farrow & Ball. Shutters, painted in Hardwick White, produced by The New England Shutter Company. **Hall:** Sofa, designed by Jannik Martensen-Larsen, produced by David Seyfried. Coffee table, designed and produced by Chelsea Textiles. Art by Kirstine Roepstorff. Wall colour, Studio Green, produced by Farrow & Ball.

SUSTAINABLE PLAYFULNESS

Office: Vintage rococo chairs, re-designed by Sarah Becker. Vintage book cabinet, via Fil de Fer. Cardboard figures, created by Shane Brox. **Living room:** Sofa, designed and produced by Christian Liegre. Lounge chairs, designed and produced by Day Home. Pillows, produced by Day Home and Zara Home. Art by Lis Kasper Bang. Trestle, via Wiingaard Boheme Interieur. Books and candlesticks, via flea market in Copenhagen. Gustav 6 Adolf of Sweden bust, via Green Square. Vintage bench, via Green Square. Vintage floor lamps, via Fil de Fer. **Dining room:** Confetti dinnerware, produced by Aluminia. Vintage glass and cutlery, via flea markets. The Ant dining chair, designed by Arne Jacobsen, produced by Fritz Hansen.

SEASIDE PEACE

Veranda: Outdoor furniture, produced by Skagerak. **Hall:** PK22 lounge chairs, designed by Poul Kjærholm, produced by Fritz Hansen. Art by Lin Utzon and Charlotte Lynggaard. **Living room:** Floyd-Hi sofa, designed by Pierro Lisoni, produced by Living Divani. Vintage table lamp, designed by Poul Henningsen, produced by Louis Poulsen. PK stool, designed by Poul Kjærholm, produced by Fritz Hansen. Vintage armchair, upholstered in fabric from GP & J Baker. **Studio:** PK52 table, designed by Poul Kjærholm, produced by Fritz Hansen. Vintage table lamp, designed by Poul Henningsen, produced by Louis Poulsen. EA 217 office chair, designed by Ray & Charles Eames, produced by Vitra. **Kitchen:** Folding chairs, designed by Mogens Koch, produced by Rud Rasmussen. Y-chair, designed by Hans J. Wegner, produced by Carl Hansen. Vintage pendant, designed by Poul Henningsen, produced by Louis Poulsen. Kitchen elements, produced by Bulthaup.

LAVISH VIBES

Living room: Module sofa, designed by Erik Rasmussen, produced by Paustian. PK 61 coffee table, designed by Poul Kjærholm, produced by Fritz Hansen. PK 22 lounge chair, designed by Poul Kjærholm, produced by Fritz Hansen. Unika chairs, created by Jay Gard, mounted on Marcel Breuer B9 frames, produced by Thonet. BL3 floor lamp, designed by Robert Dudley Best, produced by Bestlite. Kubus candlestick, designed by Mogens Lassen, produced by By Lassen. Art by Asger Dybvad Larsen, Jay Gard, Alexandre Navet, Birk Bjørlo, Christine Overvad Hansen, Lawrence Weiner, Jasper Sebastian Stürup, Amalie Jakobsen and Esben Gyldenløve, via Gether Contemporary. Bay window: AJ floor lamp, designed by Arne Jacobsen, produced by Louis Poulsen. Polka Square wallpaper, designed and produced by Farrow & Ball. Art by Robin Seir, via Gether Contemporary. **Kitchen and dining room:** Kitchen element, designed and produced by Koch Køkkener. SE68 chairs, designed by Egon Eiermann, produced by Wielde und Spieth. PK54 dining table, designed by Poul Kjærholm, produced by Fritz Hansen. Radiohus pendel, designed by Wilhelm Lauritzen, produced by Louis Poulsen. Blue fluted Plain dinnerware, produced by Royal Copenhagen. Blue Olga dinnerware, produced by Villeroy & Boch. **Hall:** The Spanish Chair, designed by Børge Mogensen, produced by Fredericia Furniture. Lamp, designed and produced by Michael Anastadiades. Vintage lamp, designed by Jean-Louis Domercq, produced by Jieldé. Art by Albert Metz, via Gether Contemporary. **Office:** MK bookcases, designed by Mogens Koch, produced by Rud Rasmussen. EA 108 office chair, designed by Ray & Charles Eames, produced by Vitra. Vintage table lamp, designed by Jean-Louis Domercq, produced by Jieldé. Boxes, designed and produced by August Sandgreen.

FLAWLESSLY AWESOME

Living room: Wall colour, Bagdad Grey, produced by Flügger. Sofa, designed and produced by Meridiani. Heritage lounge chair, designed by Frits Henningsen, produced by Carl Hansen & Son. CH008 coffee table, designed by Hans J. Wegner, produced by Carl Hansen & Son. Unique Beni Ourain rug, designed by and distributed via Mette Beck Adsbøl. **Dining room:** Dining table, designed and produced by Koch Køkkener. CH26 and CH33 dining chairs, designed by Hans J. Wegner, produced by Carl Hansen & Son. Unique walnut trays, designed by and distributed via Mette Beck Adsbøl. Unique ceramics, designed by and distributed via Mette Bech Adsbøl. Tablecloth made in fabric from GP & J Baker. VL Ring Crown 5 chandelier, designed by Vilhelm Lauritzen, produced by Louis Poulsen. Curtains, made in fabric from Society. Cone wall lamps, designed by and distribution via Mette Beck Adsbøl. **Kitchen:** Kitchen elements, designed and produced by Københavns Møbelsnedkeri. Ceiling lamp, produced by Claus Cph. **Bathroom:** Wall colour, Oregon Grape, produced by Flügger. Antique mirrors, via Fil de Fer. Bestlite wall lamps, designed by Robert Dudley Best, produced by Gubi. Unique granite sinks from Bali, mounted on cabinets produced by Københavns Møbelsnedkeri. Stone tops, produced by Made a Mano. Fixtures, produced by Toni. **Bedroom:** Bedlinen, designed and produced by Aiayu. Curtains, made in fabric fom Dedar, via Tapet-Café. Pillows, made in fabric from GP & J Baker. Bed, designed and produced by Comfort Beds.

PAPER POETRY

Kitchen: Dining table with tabletop designed by Amanda Betz, frame produced by Københavns Møbelsnedkeri. Cassiopeia lamp, designed by Amanda Betz, produced by Le Klint. Cross chairs, designed by Pearson Lloyd, produced by Takt. White Elements dinnerware, designed by Louise Cambell, produced by Royal Copenhagen. Grand Prix cutlery, designed and produced by Kay Bojesen. Nagel candlesticks, produced by Stoff Copenhagen. Napkins, produced by Cozy Living. Art, created by Eske Rex. Ceramic plate and mugs, designed and produced by Gurli Elbækgaard. Tea pot and bowl, designed and produced by Tina Marie Cph. Star sun, designed and produced by Amanda Betz. Leaves, designed and produced by Ferm Living. **Living room:** Sofa, produced by ILVA. Turnings coffee table, designed by Therese Arns, produced by Menu. Folded vase, designed by Amanda Betz, produced by Menu.

Vintage Beni Ourain Rug. Blanket, designed and produced by Roommers. Bitch lounge chair, designed and produced by Design By Us. Nelson Saucer Bubble Pendant, designed by George Nelson. Vintage floor lamp, designed and produced by Le Klint. Table lamp, designed by Sofie Refer, produced by Nuura. Paper art, created by Pernelle Caspersen. Soft bench, designed by Thomas Bentzen, produced by Takt. Vase, designed and produced by Tina Marie Cph. Art, created by Malene Landgreen. Glass balls, designed and produced by Iitalla. Advent wreath, designed and produced by Ferm Living, decorated with unika paper decorations, created by Amanda Betz. Candles, produced by Ester & Erik. **Studio:** String shelving system, designed by Niels Strinning, produced by String Furniture. Ceiling lamp, designed by Søren Rose, produced by Menu. Ikebana vase, designed by Jamie Hayon, produced by Fritz Hansen. Fragment lamp, designed by Amanda Betz. Art, created by Amanda Betz.

COLOUR COURAGE

Living room: The Tired Man, designed by Flemming Lassen, produced by By Lassen. Coffee table, produced by 101 Copenhagen. Sofa, designed and produced by ILVA. Vintage Beni Ourain rug. Blossi floor and table lamp, designed by Sofie Refer, produced by Nuura. Apiales chandelier, designed by Sofie Refer, produced by Nuura. Molekyl candlestick, designed by Michael Rem, produced by Gejst. Handmade candles, produced by Ester & Erik. Kubus candlestick, designed by Mogens Lassen, produced by By Lassen. Nebl flowerpot, designed by Micheal Rem, produced by Gejst. **Kitchen:** Kitchen elements, produced by Designovation Studio, painted in NCS S7020-R10B. Table top, produced by Borderstone. Fixture, designed and produced by Quooker. Hector dining table, designed and produced by Eberhardt Furniture. Coco dining chairs, designed and produced by Gubi. Apiales chandelier, designed by Sofie Refer, produced by Nuura. Blue Elements dinnerware, designed by Louise Campbell, produced by Royal Copenhagen. Molekyl candlestick, designed by Michael Rem, produced by Gejst. Wallpaper, designed and produced by Ferm Living. Stove, designed and produced by Morsø. **Bathroom:** New Dawn Rose wallpaper, designed by Borås tapeter, via Tapetforum. Fixture, designed and produced by Vola. Liila wall lamp, designed by Sofie Refer, produced by Nuura.

FAIRYTALE FLAIR

Living room: Art by Merete Zacho and others. Paper stars and ornaments, designed by Violise Lunn. **Office:** Dress sculptures, designed by Violise Lunn. Paper lamps, designed by Violise Lunn. Mirror in gold frame, requisition from The Royal Danish Theatre. **Kitchen:** Paper art by Louise Campbell. Vintage lamps, chairs and table. Christmas ornaments, designed by Violise Lunn, some produced by Royal Copenhagen.

CONTACTS

KATRINE MARTENSEN-LARSEN
Instagram: @katrinemartensenlarsen
website: kmldesign.dk

LEIF SIGERSEN
Instagram: @leifsigersen
website: leifsigersen.com

CATHRINE BORGE
Instagram: @bolinabolina
website: bolina.no

CAMILLA ROSÉN
Instagram: @c_ro.copenhagen
Website: c-rocopenhagen.com

HELENE BLANCHE
Instagram: @heleneblanche
website: heleneblanche.com

SHANE BROX
Instagram: @shanebrox

CHARLOTTE LYNGGAARD
Instagram: @charlottelynggaard_dk
website: olelynggaard.dk

CAMILLA AND SOPHUS GETHER
Instagram: @gether_contemporary
website: gethercontemporary.com

METTE BECK ADSBØL
Instagram: @mette_beck_adsbol_indretning

AMANDA BETZ
Instagram: @theamandabetz
website: amandabetz.com

NADIA LASSEN
Instagram: @nadialassen
website: nuura.com

VIOLISE LUNN
Instagram: @violiselunn
website: violise.dk

SOURCES

www.blixen.dk
www.christmastree.dk
www.citatfabrikken.dk
www.coolstuff.dk
www.dr.dk
www.experimentarium.dk
www.folkekirken.dk
www.historienet.dk
www.historie-online.dk
www.humanisme.dk
www.juleri.dk
www.jule-sange.dk
www.julestads.dk
www.juleweb.dk
www.julforalle.dk
www.julidannevang.dk
www.kristendom.dk
www.lenesjul.dk
www.nabokalenderne.dk
www.nrk.no
www.svt.se
www.tv2.dk
www.visitnorway.dk
www.visitsweden.dk
www.wikipedia.com
www.wikiquote.org

THE CHRISTMAS SEASON

Created by Scandinavian Artists

ISBN: 978 1 78884 325 6

First published by KML Design under the title THE SEASON CREATED BY SCANDINAVIAN ARTISTS by Katrine Martensen-Larsen

Author: Katrine Martensen-Larsen www.kmldesign.dk
Photography: Mikkel Adsbøl www.mikkeladsbol.dk
Pattern: Helene Blanche
Illustrations: Sofia Lynggaard Normann
Graphic design: Sophie Klerk
Translation: Becca Shaw Frandsen

First published by ACC Art Books by agreement with KML Design in 2021 (large format)
This edition published by ACC Art Books by agreement with KML Design in 2025

The author and publisher gratefully acknowledge the permission granted to reproduce the copyright material in this book. Every effort has been made to trace copyright holders and to obtain their permission for the use of copyright material. Any errors or omissions are entirely unintentional and should be addressed to the publisher.

A CIP record for this book is available from the British Library

EU GPSR Authorised Representative:
Easy Access System Europe Oü, 16879218
Address: Mustamäetee 50, 10621 Tallinn, Estonia
Email: gpsr@easproject.com Tel:+358 40 5003575

FSC www.fsc.org MIX Paper | Supporting responsible forestry FSC® C008047

Printed in China by C&C Offset Printing Co. Ltd
for ACC Art Books Ltd, Woodbridge, Suffolk, UK

www.accartbooks.com

ACC ART BOOKS